HARDPRESS.NET
HOME OF HARD-TO-FIND BOOKS

An Expository Outline of the 'Vestiges of the Natural History of Creation', by R. Chambers With a Notice of the Author's 'Explanations'.

by Robert Chambers

Address:
HardPress
8345 NW 66TH ST #2561
MIAMI FL 33166-2626
USA
Email: info@hardpress.net

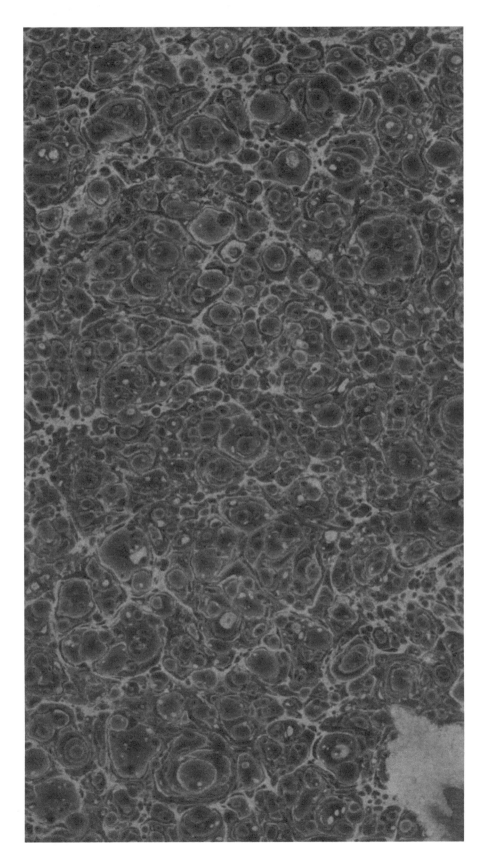

46.

79ℓ.

AN EXPOSITORY OUTLINE

OF THE

"VESTIGES OF THE NATURAL HISTORY OF CREATION."

AN

EXPOSITORY OUTLINE

OF THE

"VESTIGES OF THE
NATURAL HISTORY OF CREATION;"

WITH A COMPREHENSIVE AND CRITICAL ANALYSIS OF THE
ARGUMENTS BY WHICH THE EXTRAORDINARY HYPO-
THESES OF THE AUTHOR ARE SUPPORTED AND
HAVE BEEN IMPUGNED, WITH THEIR BEARING
UPON THE RELIGIOUS AND MORAL INTE-
RESTS OF THE COMMUNITY.

WITH A NOTICE OF THE AUTHOR'S

" EXPLANATIONS :"

A SEQUEL TO THE VESTIGES.

Originally printed in a Supplement of The Atlas *Newspaper
of August* 30 *and December* 20, 1845.

LONDON:

EFFINGHAM WILSON, ROYAL EXCHANGE.
J. VINCENT, OXFORD; G. ANDREWS, DURHAM; J. TEPPELL,
NORWICH; BRODIE AND CO., SALISBURY.
A. AND C. BLACK, EDINBURGH; D. ROBERTSON, GLASGOW;
A. BROWN AND CO., ABERDEEN.
W. CURRY, JUN., AND CO., DUBLIN.

1846.

791.

ADVERTISEMENT.

THE following tractate first appeared in the form of a literary review in a supplement of the ATLAS; but two impressions of that journal having been long since exhausted, and inquiries still continuing numerous and urgent, the proprietor has granted permission for the article to be reprinted in a separate, more convenient, and perhaps enduring vehicle than that of a newspaper.

Few works of a scientific import have been published that so promptly and deeply fixed public attention as the *Vestiges of Creation*, or elicited more numerous replies and sharper critical analysis and disquisition. Upon so vast a question as the evolution of universal creation differences of opinion were natural and unavoidable. Many have disputed the accuracy of some of the author's facts, and the sequence and validity of his inductive inferences; but few can withhold from him the praise of a patient and intrepid spirit of inquiry, much occasional eloquence, and very considerable powers of analysis, systematic induction, arrangement and combination.

In what follows the leading objects kept in view have been—first, an expository outline of the author's facts and argument; next, of the chief reasons by which they have been impugned by Professor SEDGWICK, Professor WHEWELL, Mr. BOSANQUET, and others who have entered the lists of controversy. These arrayed, the concluding purpose fitly followed of a brief exhibition of the relative strength of the main points in issue, with their bearing on the moral and religious interests of the community.

It is the fourth and latest edition that has been submitted to investigation. In this impression the author has introduced several corrections and alterations, without, however, any infringement or mitigation of its original scope and character. More recently appeared his "Explanations," a Sequel to the "Vestiges of the Natural History of Creation;" in which the author endeavours to elucidate and strengthen his former position. This had become necessary in consequence of the number of his opponents, and the inquiry and discussion to which the original publication had given rise. Of this, also, a lengthened review was given in the ATLAS, which has been included; so that the reader will now have before him a succinct outline of a novel and interesting topic of philosophical investigation.

In the present reprint a few corrections have been made, and the illustrative table at page 34, and some other additions, introduced.

London, January 1, 1846.

AN EXPOSITORY OUTLINE

OF THE

"VESTIGES OF THE NATURAL HISTORY OF CREATION."

It rarely happens that speculative inquiries in England command much attention, and the *Vestiges of Creation* would have probably formed no exception, had it not been from the unusual ability with which the work has been executed. The subject investigated is one of vast, almost universal, interest; for everyone—the low, in common with the high in intellect—find enigmas in creation that they would gladly have unriddled, and promptly gather round the oracle who has boldly stepped forth to cut the knot of their perplexities. The first impression made, too, is favourable. No very striking originality, eloquence, or genius, is displayed; yet there is ingenuity; and though the author betrays the zeal of an advocate, desirous of leading to a determinate and *material* conclusion, his address, like that of the apostle of temperance, is mostly mild and equable, with occasionally a little gentlemanly fervour to give animation to his discourse. His style is mostly felicitous, sometimes beautiful, lucid, precise, and elevated. In tone and manner of execution, in quiet steadiness of purpose, in the firm, intrepid spirit with which truth, or that which is conceived to be true, is followed, regardless of startling presentments, the *Vestiges* call to mind the *Mécanique Céleste*, or *Système du Monde*. In caution, as in science, the author is immeasurably inferior to LAPLACE; but in magnitude and boldness of design he transcends the illustrious Frenchman. LAPLACE sought no more than to subject the celestial movements to the formulas of analysis, and reconcile to common observation terrestrial appearances; but our author is far more ambitious—more venturesome in aim—which is nothing less than to lift the veil of Isis, and solve the phenomena of universal nature. With what success remains to be considered. That great skill and cleverness, that a very superior mastery is evinced, we have conceded, and, we will also add, great show of fairness in treatment and conclusion.

No partial opening is made; the great design, in all its extent, is manfully grappled with. The universe is first surveyed, next the mystery of its origin. After ranging through sidereal space, examining the bodies found there, their arrangement, formation, and evolution, the author selects our own planet for especial interrogation. He disembowels it, scrutinizing the internal evidences of its structure and history, and thence infers the causes of past vicissitudes, existing relations, and appearances. These disposed of, the surface is explored, the phenomena of animal and vegetable existence contemplated, and the sources of vital action, sexual differences, and diversities of species assigned. Man, as the supreme head and last work of progressive creation, challenges a distinct consideration; his history and mental constitution are investigated, and the relation in which a sublime reason stands to the instinct of brutes discriminated. The end and purpose of all appropriately form the concluding theme, which finished, the curtain drops, and the last sounds heard are that the name of the Great Unknown will probably never be revealed; that " praise will elicit no response," nor any " word of censure" be parried or deprecated.

" Give me," exclaimed ARCHIMEDES, " a fulcrum, and I will raise the earth." " Give me," says the author of the *Vestiges*, " gravitation and development, and I will create a universe." ALEXANDER'S ambition was to conquer a world, our author's is to create one. But he is wrong in saying that his is the " first attempt to connect the natural sciences into a history of creation, and thence to eliminate a view of nature as one grand system of causation." The attempt has been often made, but utterly failed; its results have been found valueless, hurtful—to have occupied without enlarging the intellect, and the very effort has long been discountenanced. Great advances, however, have been made in science since system-making began to be discredited; nature has been perseveringly ransacked in all her domains, and many extraordinary secrets drawn from her laboratory. Astronomy and geology, chemistry and electricity, have greatly extended the bounds of knowledge; still, we apprehend, we are not yet sufficiently armed with facts to resolve into one consistent whole her infinite variety.

Efforts at generalization, however, and the systematic arrangement of natural phenomena, are seldom wholly fruitless. If false, they tend to provoke discussion—to lead to active thought and useful research. A solitary truth, though new and useful, rarely obtains higher distinction than to be quietly placed on the rolls of science, while a bold speculation, traversing the whole field of creation, and smoothing all its difficulties, satisfies for the moment, and fixes general attention. Of this the *Vestiges of Creation* are an example. Without adding to our positive knowledge by a single new discovery, demonstration, or experiment, they have excited more interest than the *Principia* of NEWTON. From this popular success, if good do not accrue, no great evil need be anticipated. Hypotheses are most hurtful when accredited by an irreversible authority—when erected into a tribunal without appeal, they become the arbitrary dictator in lieu of the handmaid of science. Discussion and invention, in place of being stimulated, are then fettered by them; the human mind is enslaved, as Europe was for centuries by the *Physics* of ARISTOTLE, and still continues to be in some of the ancient retreats and conservatories of exploded errors. But these form the exceptions, not the rule of the age, which is free and equal inquiry. Errors have ceased to have prescriptive immunities; and mere conjectures, however sanctioned or plausible, if inconsistent with science—with the ascertained facts of experiment and observation, are speedily passed into the region of dreams and chimeras.

Whether this will be the fate of our author remains to be proved. The moment selected for his appearance has at least been well chosen. The *Vestiges* have the air of novelty, a long time having elapsed since any one had the hardihood to propound a new system of Nature. In common with most manifestations of our time, his effort exhibits a marked improvement on the crudities of his predecessors in the same line of architectural ambition. Science has been called to his aid, and the patient ingenuity with which he has sought to make the latest discoveries subservient to his purpose challenges admiration, if not acquiescence. Some of our contemporaries have been warmed into almost theological aversion by the boldness of his conclusions, but we see little cause for fear, and none for bitterness or apprehension. More closely Nature is investigated and deeper the impression will become of her majesty and might. Unlike earthly greatnesses, she loses no power—no grandeur—no fascination—no prestige, by familiarity. The greatest philosophers will always rank among her greatest admirers and most devout and fervent worshippers.

Had our author proved all he has assumed our faith would not be lessened, nor our wonder diminished. Whether matter or spirit has been the world's architect, the astounding miracle of its creation is not the less. What does it import whether it resulted direct from the fiat of Omnipotence, or intermediately from the properties He impressed, or the law of development He prescribed? He who gave the law, who infused the energies by which Chaos was transmuted into an organized universe, remains great and inscrutable as ever.

It is time, however, that we entered upon a more detailed and closer investigation of the *Vestiges of Creation.* Our purpose is not hastily, and without examination, to deprecate, deny, or controvert; but patiently, and without prejudice, to inquire, to submit faithfully and intelligibly the outlines of a remarkable treatise; describe briefly its scope and bearing, the arguments by which they are supported, and the counter reasons by which they appear to be wholly or partially impugned. Our readers will thus be enabled to appreciate the merits of a controversy, the most comprehensive and interesting that for a lengthened period has occupied the attention of the scientific and intellectual world.

For greater clearness of exposition we shall endeavour to follow the order observed by the author in the division and treatment of his subjects, commencing first with the

BODIES OF SPACE.

The author opens his subject with a brief but luminous outline of the arrangement and formation of the astral and planetary systems of the heavens. He first describes the solar system, of which our earth is a member, consisting of the sun, planets, and satellites with the less intelligible orbs termed comets, and taking as the uttermost bounds of this system the orbit of Uranus, it occupies a portion of space not less than three thousand six hundred millions of miles in diameter. The mind cannot form an exact notion of so vast an expanse, but an idea of it may be obtained from the fact, that, if the swiftest racehorse ever known had began to traverse it at full speed at the time of the birth of MOSES, he would only yet have accomplished half his journey. Vast as is the solar system, it is only one of an infinity of others which may be still more extensive. Our sun is supposed to be a star belonging to a constellation of stars, each of which has its accompaniment of revolving planets; and the constellation itself with similar constellations to form revolving clusters round some mightier centre of attraction; and so on, each astral combination increasing in number, magnitude, and complexity, till the mind is utterly lost in the vain effort to grasp the limitless arrangement.

Of the stars astronomers can hardly be said to know anything with certainty. Sirius, which is the most lustrous, was long supposed to be the nearest and most within the reach of observation, but all attempts to calculate the distance of that luminary have proved futile. Of its inconceivable remoteness some notion may be formed by the fact, that the diameter of the earth's annual orbit, if viewed from it, would dwindle into an invisible point. This is what is meant by the stars not having, like the planets, a *parallax;* that is, the earths' orbit, as seen from them, does not subtend a measurable angle. With two other stars, however, astronomers have unexpectedly and recently been more fortunate than with Sirius, and have been able to calculate their distances from the earth. The celebrated BESSEL, and soon afterwards, the late Mr. HENDERSON, astronomer royal for Scotland, were the first to surmount the difficulty that had baffled the telescopic resources of the HERSCHELS. BESSEL detected a parallax of one-third of a second in the star 61 Cygni, and in the constellation of the Centaur HENDERSON found another star whose parallax amounted to one second. Of the million of fixed glittering points that adorn the sky, these are the only two whose distances have been calculated, and to express them, miles, leagues, or orbits seems inadequate. Light, whose speed is known to be 192,000 miles per second, would be three years in reaching our earth from the star of HENDERSON ; and starting from BESSEL's star and moving at the same rate it could only reach us in ten years.   These are the nearest stars, but there are others whose distances are immeasurably greater, and whose light, though starting from them at the beginning of creation, may not have reached our globe !

The stars visible to the eye are about 3,000, but the number increases with every increase of telescopic power, and may be said to be innumerable.   They are not of uniform lustre or form, but vary in figure and brightness.   Some of them have a *nebulous* or cloudy appearance ;   and there are entire clusters with this dusky aspect, mostly pervaded, however, with luminous points of more brilliant hue.   In the outer fields of astral space Sir WILLIAM HERSCHEL observed a multitude of nebulæ, one or two of which may be seen by the naked eye.   All of them, when seen by instruments of low power, look like masses of luminous vapour; but some of them had brighter spots, suggesting to Sir WILLIAM the idea of a condensation of the nebulous matter round one or more centres.   But when these luminous masses are examined by more powerful instruments many of them lose their cloudy form, and are resolved into shining points, "like spangles of diamond dust."   It is in this way several nebulæ have yielded to the gigantic reflector of Lord ROSSE, and others with still greater optical resources may follow.   This brings us to the first questionable and controversial portion of the *Vestiges ;* namely,—the

NEBULAR HYPOTHESIS.

It is among the gaseous bodies just described, in the outer boundary of Nature, which neither telescope nor geometry can well reach, that speculation has laid its *venue*, and commenced its aerial castles.   LAPLACE was the first to suggest the nebular hypothesis, which he did with great diffidence, not as a theory proved, or hardly likely, but as a mathematical possibility or illustration.   His range of creation, moreover, was not so vast as that of our author, which assumes to compass the entire uni-verse, but was limited to the evolution of the solar system.   The mode in which this might be evolved, LAPLACE thus explains :—

He conjectures that in the original condition of the solar system the sun revolved upon his axis, surrounded by an atmosphere which, in virtue of an excessive heat, extended far beyond the orbits of all the planets, the planets as yet having no existence. The heat gradually diminished, and as the solar atmosphere contracted by cooling, the rapidity of its rotation increased by the laws of rotatory motion, and an exterior zone of vapour was detached from the rest, the central attraction being no longer able to overcome the increased centrifugal force. The zone of vapour might in some cases retain its form, as we still see in Saturn's ring; but more usually the ring of vapour would break into several masses, and these would generally coalesce into one mass, which would revolve about the sun. Such portions of the solar atmosphere abandoned successively at different distances, would form planets in the state of vapour. These masses of vapour, it appears from mechanical laws, would have each its rotatory motion, and as the cooling of the vapour still went on, would each produce a planet that might have satellites and rings formed from the planet, in the same manner as the planets were formed from the atmosphere of the sun.

All the known motions of the solar system are consistent and reconcileable with this theory of LAPLACE, and upon it the author of the *Vestiges* has enlarged and founded his wider scheme of physical creation. He supposes the void of nature to have been originally filled with a universal FIRE MIST (p. 30), out of which all the celestial orbs were made and put in motion. How this mist was put in activity, and resolved into the luminous and revolving bodies that we now see, and one of which we inhabit is the first urgent perplexity to surmount in the conjecture. It is manifest that if a mist filled the entire region of space, a mist it must for ever remain, unless acted upon by some cause adequate to give it new action and arrangement. No sun, no stars or planets could spontaneously emanate from an inert vapour any more than from nothing. To meet this, his first difficulty, the author supposes that there were certain *nuclei*, or centres of greater condensation, analogous to those still remarked in the nebulæ of the heavens, and that these nuclei, by their superior attractive force, consolidated into spheres the gaseous matter around them :—

"Of nebulous matter," says he, "in its original state we know too little to enable us to suggest *how nuclei should be established in it.* But supposing that from a *peculiarity* in the constitution nuclei are formed, we know very well how, by the power of gravitation, the process of an aggregation of the neighbouring matter to these nuclei should proceed until masses more or less solid should be detached from the rest. It is a *well-known law in physics, that when fluid matter collects towards, or meets in a centre, it establishes a rotatory motion.* See minor results of this law in the whirlpool and the whirlwind—nay, on so humble a scale as the water sinking through the aperture of a funnel. It thus becomes certain, that when we arrive at the stage of a nebulous star we have a rotation on its axis commenced."

Up to this, however, the author has proved nothing. The existence of the fire-mist and nuclei are assumptions only, and the way by which he tries to account for rotatory motion is clearly erroneous. The aggregation of matter round the nuclei by gravitation would have no such tendency; no more than a perfect balance would of itself have a tendency to move about its fulcrum, or a falling stone to deviate from its vertical course. Gravitation would indeed compress the particles of matter, but its tendency and entire action is towards the nucleus; it compresses them no more on one side of the line of their direction to the centre of force than on any other side; and hence no *lateral* or *rotatory motion* would ensue. Rotation, therefore, is yet unaccounted for; though the author says *it is a well-known law in physics* that when fluid matter collects towards, or meets in a centre, it establishes a rotatory motion; and then for illustration refers to a whirlwind or whirlpool. No such effect would follow the conditions stated, and an entire ignorance is betrayed of the laws of mechanical philosophy. In the whirlpool and the whirlwind the gyration is caused by the fluid passing, not *to* the centre, but *through* it and away from it; in the whirlpool downwards through the place of exit, in the whirlwind upwards to where the vacuum has caused the rapid aggregation.

LAPLACE was too able a mathematician to commit these elementary blunders; he did not assume to account for rotation by inapplicable laws, but took for granted that the sun revolved upon its axis, and thence communicated a corresponding motion to the bodies thrown from its surface. But our author has sought to advance beyond his teacher, and in this way has shown his ignorance of physics by an egregious mistake. At this point we might stop, without following the ulterior steps by which the solar system is made to evolve out of heated vapour. Having got rotation, though by an impossible process, the author falls into the illustration already given of the theory of LAPLACE. The rotation of each nucleus or sun round its axis produces centrifugal force ; that force, by refrigeration, increases beyond the centripetal force of gravity ; in consequence rings are formed and detached from the surface, whose unequal coherence of parts mostly causes them to break into separate masses or planets, partaking of the motion of the bodies from which they have been separated, and these primaries in their turn becoming centres of gravitation and centrifugal force, throw off their secondaries, or moons.

In this way the solar system and other systems upon a similar plan of arrangement, it is conjectured, may have been formed. According to the author the generative process is still in progress, and new worlds are in course of being thrown off from new suns in the confines of creation. These nebulous stars on the outer bounds of space, of varying forms and brightness, are supposed to be the centres of new systems in different stages of development, like children of various ages and growth in a numerous family. This is the author's own illustration (p. 20), and after giving it he proceeds :—

"Precisely thus, seeing in our astral system many thousands of worlds in all stages of formation, from the most rudimental to that immediately preceding the present condition of those] we deem perfect, it is unavoidable to conclude that all the perfect have gone through the various stages which we see in the rudimental. This leads us at once to the conclusion that the whole of our firmament was at one time a diffused mass of nebulous matter, extending through the space which it still occupies. So also, of *course*, must have been the other astral systems. Indeed, we must presume the whole to have been originally in one connected mass, the astral systems being only the first division into parts, and solar systems the second.

" The first idea which all this impresses upon us is, that the formation of bodies in space is *still and at present in progress*. [We live at a time when many have been formed, and many are still forming. Our own solar system is to be regarded as completed, supposing its perfection to consist in the formation of a series of planets, for there are mathematical reasons for concluding that Mercury is the nearest planet to the sun, which can, according to the laws of the system, exist. But there are other solar systems within our astral systems, which are as yet in a less advanced state, and even some quantities of nebulous matter which have scarcely begun to advance towards the stellar form. On the other hand, there are vast numbers of stars which have all the appearance of being fully formed systems, if we are to judge from the complete and definite appearance which they present to our vision through the telescope. We have no means of judging of the *seniority of systems; but it is reasonable to suppose that among the many, some are older than ours.* There is, indeed, one piece of evidence for the probability of the comparative youth of our system, altogether apart from human traditions and the geognostic appearances of the surface of our planet. This consists in a thin nebulous matter, which is diffused around the sun to nearly the orbit of Mercury, of a very oblately spheroidal shape. This matter, which sometimes appears to our naked eyes, at sunset, in the form of a cone projecting upwards in the line of the sun's path, and which bears the name of the Zodiacal Light, has been thought a residuum or last remnant of the concentrating matter of our system, and thus may be supposed to indicate the comparative recentness of the principal events of our cosmogony. *Supposing the surmise and inference* to be correct, and they may be held as so far supported by more familiar evidence, we might with the more confidence speak of our system as not amongst the elder born of Heaven, but one whose various phenomena, physical and moral, as yet lay undeveloped, while myriads of others were fully fashioned, and in complete arrangement. Thus, in the sublime chronology to which we are directing our inquiries, we first find ourselves called upon to consider the globe which we inhabit as a child of the sun, elder than Venus and her younger brother Mercury, but posterior in date of birth to Mars, Jupiter, Saturn, and Uranus; next to regard our whole system as probably of recent formation in comparison with many of the stars of our firmament. We must, however, be on our guard against supposing the earth as a recent globe in our ordinary conceptions of time. From evidence afterwards to be adduced, it will be seen that it cannot be presumed to be less than many hundreds of centuries old. How much older Uranus may be, no one can tell, far less how much more aged may be many of the stars of our firmament, or the stars of other firmaments, than ours."

All this is ingenious and fluently expressed. The author has an easy way of surmounting his difficulties by the use of such little auxiliary phrases, as "of course," "it may be surmised," "it is reasonable to suppose," and so on; which, though trifling in themselves, help him in their connecting inferences through many embarrassing perplexities. But his hypothesis is yet unproved; his fire-mist is only a conjecture; his nuclei, scattered like so many eggs in space out of which future suns and worlds are in process of incubation, is of the same description, and rotation, the first step in his process of creation, would not ensue under the conditions he has assigned. Without dwelling on these short-comings, we shall terminate this portion of the author's inquiry with a few general strictures. First, on its inconsistency with what we know of the solar system; and, secondly, on its in-adequacy to explain the facts of which we are cognizant on our own globe.

In the first place, for the hypothesis to be applicable to our system, it is requisite that the primary and secondary bodies should revolve, both in their orbits and round their axes, in one direction, and nearly in one plane. Most of the bodies of the system observe these laws, their orbits are nearly circular, nearly in the plane of the original equator of the solar rotation, and in the direction of that rotation. But there are exceptions; the comets, which intersect the equatorial plane in every angle of direction form one, and the most distant of the planets forms another. The satellites of Uranus are retrograde. They move from east to west in orbits highly inclined to that of their pri-mary, and on both accounts are exceptions to the order of the other secondary bodies. Our author is so perplexed by this in-consistency that he first doubts the fact, and next tries to explain it by alleging that " it may be owing to a *bouleversement* of the primary." What is meant by the *bouleversement* of a planet none of his critics seem to apprehend, nor do we. But that the moons of Uranus are contrariwise to those of the other planets, Sir JOHN HERSCHEL has indubitably established; so that the author at any rate upon this point has sustained a bouleversement.

Our own moon forms a third exception to his theory. Ac-cording to his system, this satellite is a slip or graft from our planet, and in constitution, it might be inferred, would partake of the elements of the parent. But the fact is otherwise. The moon has no atmosphere, no seas, or rivers, nor any water, and

B

of course totally unfit for human inhabitants, or organic life of any kind. It must, then, have had a different origin, or be in some earlier stage of development than that through which our earth has passed.

Leaving these exceptions, we may next inquire into the relevant purposes of the nebular hypothesis, supposing its assumptions acquiesced in. Like the fanciful theories of the ancient philosophers, it seems only to involve a profitless topic of controversy, without solving natural phenomena. It does not unravel the mystery of the beginning, brings us no nearer to the first creative force. Like a good chemist, previous to analysis, the author first throws all matter into a state of solution; but granting him his fire-mist and nuclei in the midst, how or whence came this condition and arrangement of nature? What was its pre-existing state? or, if that be answered, how or whence was that preceding state educed, for it, too, must have had one prior to it? So that the mind makes no advances by such inquiries, is lost in a maze that can have no end, because it has no beginning; and, like Noah's messenger, for want of a resting place, is compelled to return to the first starting point. Easier, and quite as satisfactory, it seems to believe, as we have been taught to believe, that the celestial spheres were at once perfect and entire, projected into space from the hands of the maker, than that they were elaborated out of luminous vapour by gravity and condensation. Hopeless inquiry is thus foreclosed, an inquisition that cannot be answered, silenced, and removed out of the pale of discussion.

It is not from any attribute of the Deity being impugned that the hypothesis is objectionable. Design and intelligence in the creation are left paramount as before, and our impression of the skill exercised, and the means employed, only transferred to another part of the work. He who produced the primordial condition the author supposes, who filled space with such a mist, composed of such materials, subjected to such laws, such constitution, that sun, moon, and stars necessarily resulted from them, appears omnipotent as ever. But it does not advance inquiry, nor assist us in explaining the wonders we contemplate in our own globe. Suppose a planet formed by the author's process, what kind of a body would it be? Something, as Professor WHE-

WELL suggests, resembling a large meteoric stone. How after wards came this unformed mass to be like our earth, to be covered with motion and organization, with life and general felicity? What primitive cause stocked it with plants and animals, and produced all the surprising and subtle contrivances which we find in their structure, all the wide and profound mutual dependence which we trace in their economy? Is it possible to conceive, as the *Vestiges* inculcate, that man, with his sentiment and intellect, his powers and passions, his will and conscience, were also produced as the ultimate result of vapourous condensation?

One more conjecture of the author, in this division of his subject, we shall only notice. It is that " the formation of bodies in space *is still in progress.*" What may be doing in the nebulæ, in the region scarcely within reach of telescopic vision, in what may be considered the yet uninclosed and commonable waste of the universe, is a subject, we suspect, of much obscurity, and respecting which no precise intelligence has been received ; but limiting attention to the solar system, which is nearer home and more within cognizance, the work seems finished, perfect, and unchangeable, and, like the Great Architect, made to endure for ever. This was the conclusion of LAPLACE ; he proved that the state of our system is *stable;* that is, the ellipsis the planets describe will always remain nearly circular, and the axis of revolution of the earth will never deviate much from its present position. He also gave a mathematical proof that this stability is not accidental, but the result of design, of an arrangement by which the planets all move in the same direction, in orbits of small eccentricity and slightly inclined to each other. Reasoning from analogy, as the author of the *Vestiges* is prone to do—extending our views from our solar system to other systems— other suns and revolving planets—it is fair to conclude that they are not less perfect in arrangement—subject to like conditions of permanency, and alike exempt from mutation, decay, collision, or extinction.

Descending from this high region, we accompany the author to his next and lower field—the

EARTH AND ITS GEOLOGICAL HISTORY.

Our globe is somewhat less than 8,000 miles in diameter; it is of a spheroidal form, the equatorial exceeding the polar axis in the proportion of 300 to 299, and which slight inequality, in consequence of its diurnal revolution, is necessary to preserve the land near the equator from inundation by the sea. The mean density or average weight of the earth is, in proportion to that of distilled water, as 5.66 to 1. So that its specific gravity is considerably less than that of tin, the lightest of the metals, but exceeds that of granite, which is three times heavier than water.

Descending below the surface, the first sensation that strikes is the increase of temperature. This is so rapid, that for every one hundred feet of sinking we obtain an increase of more than one degree of Fahrenheit's thermometer. If there be no interruption to this law, and no reason exists to conclude there is, it is manifest that at the depth of a few miles we must reach an intensity of heat utterly unbearable. Hence it follows that by no improvements in machinery can mining operations be carried down to a great depth below the surface. The greatest depth yet penetrated does not exceed three thousand feet, and forms a very small advance towards the earth's centre, distant 4,000 miles.

Geologists, however, without penetrating far into the earth, have found means for obtaining an insight for several miles into its interior structure, and armed with hammer, chisel, and climbing hook, they explore the beetling sea-cliff, traverse the deepest valleys, and scale the highest mountains, carefully examining their formation, disposition, and substance, and are thus enabled to obtain some knowledge of the earth's stomach, as it were, by scrutinising the deposits and eruptive ejectments on its surface. For example, we come to a mountain composed of a particular substance with strata or beds of other rock lying against its sloped sides; we, of course, infer that the substance of the mountain dips away under the strata that we see lying against it. Suppose that we walk away from the mountain across the turned-up edges of the stratified rocks, and that for many miles we continue to pass over other stratified rocks, all disposed in the same way, till we begin to cross the opposite edges of the same beds;

after which we pass over these rocks all in reverse order, till we come to another extensive mountain composed of similar materials to the first, and shelving away under the strata in the same way; we should then infer that the stratified rocks occupied a basin formed by the rocks of these two mountains, and by calculating the thickness right through these strata could say to what depths the rock of the mountain extended below. In this way has the interior of the globe been examined, and its contents and arrangement, for several miles below the surface, ascertained. The result of such inspection we leave the author of the *Vestiges* to describe :—

"It appears that the basis rock of the earth, as it may be called, is of hard texture, and crystalline in its constitution. Of this rock, granite may be said to be the type, though it runs into many varieties. Over this, except in the comparatively few places where it projects above the general level in mountains, other rocks are disposed in sheets or strata, with the appearance of having been deposited originally from water. But these last rocks have nowhere been allowed to rest in their original arrangement. Uneasy movements from below have broken them up in great inclined masses, while in many cases there has been projected through the rents rocky matter more or less resembling the great inferior crystalline mass. This rocky matter must have been in a state of fusion from heat at the time of its projection, for it is often found to have run into and filled up lateral chinks in these rents. There are even instances where it has been rent again, and a newer melted matter of the same character sent through the opening. Finally, in the crust as thus arranged, there are, in many places, chinks containing veins of metal. Thus, there is first a great inferior mass, composed of crystalline rock, and probably resting immediately on the fused and expanded matter of the interior : next, layers or strata of aqueous origin ; next, irregular masses of melted inferior rock that have been sent up volcanically and confusedly at various times amongst the aqueous rocks, breaking up these into masses, and tossing them out of their original levels."

This, we believe, is a correct outline of the crust of the earth, so far as it has been possible to observe it. It exhibits extraordinary signs of commotion and vicissitude; the lowest rocks indicating a previous condition of igneous fusion ; those above them of aqueous solution. Fire and water have thus been the chief tellurian anarchists, and the shaking of continents and the con-

stant shifting of level in sea and land still continue to attest their
restless energies. That igneous matter has, during many periods,
been protruded from below—that mountains have risen in succession from the sea, and injected their molten substance through
cracks and fissures of superincumbent strata—are facts resting on
indubitable evidence. Many masses of granite became the solid
bottom of some portions of the sea before the secondary strata
were laid gradually upon them. The granite of Mont Blanc rose
uring a recent tertiary period. "We can prove," says Professor
SEDGWICK, "more than mere shiftings of level, and that many
portions of sea and land have entirely changed their places. The
rocks at the top of Snowdon are full of petrified sea-shells; the
same may be said of some high crests of the Alps, Pyrenees, and
Andes. We have proof demonstrative that many parts of Scotland, and that all England, formed, during many ages, the solid
bottom of the sea. It may be true that the antagonist powers of
nature during the human period have reached a kind of balance.
But during all geological periods there have been such long intervals of repose, or of such gradual movements, that we may
trace the history of the earth in the successive deposits formed in
the waters of the sea." This is the great business of geology.

Although at first sight the interior of the earth appears a con-
fused scene, after careful observation we readily detect in it a
regularity and order from which much instructive light is thrown
on its past vicissitudes. The deposition of the aqueous rocks
and the projection of the volcanic have unquestionably taken
place since the settlement of the earth in its present form. They
are, indeed, of an order of events which are going on under the
agency of intelligible causes, down to the present day. We may
therefore consider these generally as recent transactions. But
advancing to the far distant antecedent era of its existence, we
may consider it to have been a globe of its present size enveloped
in the crystalline rock already described, with the waters of the
present seas and the present atmosphere around it, though these
were probably in considerably different conditions, both as to
temperature and their constituent materials, from what they now
are. We may thus presume that, without this primitive case of
granitic texture, the great bulk of the matters of our earth were
agglomerated, whether in a fluid or solid state is uncertain; but

there cannot be any doubt that they continue to exist in a condition of great heat and compression, having a mean density of more than double that of the minerals on the surface.

Judging from the results and still observable conditions, it may be inferred that the heat retained in the interior of the globe was more intense, or had greater freedom to act, in some places than in others. These become the scenes of volcanic operations, and in time marked their situations by the extrusion from below of trap and basalts—rocks composed of the crystalline matter, fused by intense heat, and developed on the surface in various conditions, according to the particular circumstances under which it was sent up; some, for example, being thrown up under water, and some in the open air, which contingencies would make considerable difference in its texture and appearance. It would, however, be a mistake to infer that, previous to these eruptions, the earth was a smooth ball, with air and water playing round it. Geology tells us plainly that there were great irregularities—lofty mountains, interspersed with deep seas—and by which, perhaps, the mountains were wholly or partially covered. But it is a fact worthy of observation that the solids of our globe cannot for a moment be exposed to water or the atmosphere without becoming liable to change. They instantly begin to wear down. The matter so worn off being carried into the neighbouring depths and there deposited, became the components of the successive series of stratified rocks, extending from the basal envelope of granite to the earth's surface, and which it will be proper briefly to describe.

DEPOSITS OR ROCK FORMATIONS.

The first of the series is the *Gneis and Mica Slate System*, of which examples are exposed to view in the Highlands of Scotland and the west of England. These earliest stratified rocks contain no matters which are not to be found in the primitive granite. They are the same in material—silica, mica, quartz, or hornblende—but changed into new forms and combinations, and hence called by Mr. Lyell metamorphic rocks. Some of them are composed exclusively of one of the materials of granite ; the

mica schist, for example, of mica ; the *quartz rocks,* of quartz.
In the metamorphic rocks no organic remains have been found,
and they are geologically below all the rocks that do contain
traces of animal life.

From the primary rocks we pass into the next ascending
series, called the *Clay Slate and Grauwacke Slate System,* which
in some places is found resting immediately on the granite, the
antecedent bed being there wanting.   This deposit has been well
examined, because some of its slate beds have been extensively
quarried for domestic purposes.   By some geologists it is called
the *Silurian System,* it being largely developed at the surface of a
district of western England formerly occupied by the Silures.
It is found also in North Wales and in the north of England, in
beds of great thickness, and in Scotland, but there the Silurian
rocks are more feebly represented.

The *Old Red Sandstone, or Devonian System,* comes next. It
forms the material of the grand and rugged mountains which
fringe many parts of our Highland coasts, and ranges, on the
south flank of the Grampians, from the eastern to the western sea
of Scotland.   There is no part of geology and science more clear
than that which refers to the ages of mountains.   It is as certain
that the Grampian mountains are older than the Alps and Apen-
nines, as it is that civilisation had reached Italy and enabled her
to subdue the world, while Scotland was the abode o. barbarism.
The Pyrenees, Carpathians, and other ranges of continental Europe are all younger than these Scotch hills, or even the insigni-
ficant Mendip Hills of southern England. Stratification tells this
tale as plainly, and more truly, than LIVY tells the story of the
Roman republic.   It tells us that at the time when the Grampians sent streams and detritus to straits where now the valleys
of the Forth and Clyde meet, the greater part of Europe was a
wide ocean.

The last three series of strata contain the remains of the earliest occupants of the globe, and of which we shall soon speak.
They are of enormous thickness—in England, not much less than
30,000 feet, or nearly six miles.

We have now arrived at the secondary rocks, of which the
lowest group is the *Carboniferous Formation,* so called from its
remarkable feature of numerous interspersed beds of coal.   It

commences with beds of the mountain limestone, which in England attains a depth of 800 yards. Coal is altogether composed of the matter of a terrestrial vegetation, transmuted by putrefaction of a peculiar kind beneath the surface of water, and in the absence of air. From examples seen at the present day at the mouths of such rivers as the Mississippi, which traverse extensive sylvan regions, it is thought that the vegetation, the rubbish of decayed forests, was carried by rivers into estuaries, and there accumulated into vast natural rafts, until it sank to the bottom, where an overlayer of sand or mud would prepare it for becoming a stratum of coal. Others conceive that the vegetation first went into the condition of peat moss, that a sink in a level then exposed it to be overrun by the sea and covered with a layer of sand or mud; that a subsequent uprise made the mud dry land, and fitted it to bear a new forest, which afterwards, like its predecessors, became a bed of peat—that, in short, by repetitions of this process the alternate layers of coal, sand and shell constituting the carboniferous group were formed.

The *Magnesian Limestone* deposits succeed the carboniferous, and sometimes pass into them by insensible gradations. In the south of England they are represented by conglomerates, and partly composed of the solid and more or less rounded fragments of the older strata. They afford a proof of what geologists have often occasion to remark of the long periods of time during which the ancient works of nature were perfected; for the older rocks were solid as they are now, and their organic remains petrified at the time these conglomerates were forming.

We can only briefly glance at the remaining chapters of geological history. The *New Red Sandstone* forms the base of the great central plains of England, and is surmounted by the oliferous marls and red arenaceous beds which pass under the succession of great oolitic terraces that stretch across England from the coasts of Dorsetshire to the north-eastern coast of Yorkshire. It marks the commencement of an important era, being the strata in which land animals are first found. The *Oolite System* which follows marks the beginning of mammalia, and in some of its beds in Buckinghamshire are found the exuviæ of tropical trees. Near Weymouth, in the well-known dirt beds, are found trees with their siliified trunks growing up in the position of nature, and their roots embedded in the soil on which they grew.

Next we have the chalk or *Cretaceous Formation*, that makes such a conspicuous figure in England. The celebrated cliffs of Dover are of this era. It forms a stripe from Yorkshire to Kent, and is found in France, Germany, Russia, and in North America. The English chalk beds are 1,200 feet thick, showing the considerable depth of the ocean in which they were formed. Their origin has been a questionable topic; they were thought to be formed from the detritus of coral reefs, but Professor EHREN-BERG has recently announced, as the result of his microscopical researches, that chalk is composed partly of inorganic particles and partly of shells of inconceivable minuteness, a cubic inch of the substance containing about ten millions of them.

In the hollows of the chalk-beds have been formed series of strata—clay, limestone, marl alternating—to which the name of the *Tertiary System* has been given. It is irregularly distributed over vast surfaces of all our continents, and must be considered as the beds of estuaries left at the conclusion of the cretaceous period. London and Paris rest on basins of this formation, and another such basin extends from near Winchester under South-ampton, and reappears in the Isle of Wight.

We hasten upward to the *Diluvial System*, which brings us near to the present surface. To this era is referred the erratic blocks, or gigantic boulder stones, which have been driven by floods across our continents, or drifted in icebergs over valleys, and perched sometimes on mountain tops. To it also must be referred the *till* of Scotland and the great brown clay of England, and our vast beds of gravel and superficial rubbish, connected with the deluvium in the history of *ossiferous caverns*, of which that examined by Dr. BUCKLAND at Kirkdale is an example. They occur in the calcareous strata, as the great caverns gene-rally do, and have in all instances been naturally closed up till the period of their discovery. At Kirkdale the remains of twenty-four species of animals were found—namely, pigeon, lark, raven, duck, partridge, mouse, water-rat, rabbit, hare, hippopotamus, rhinoceros, elephant, weasel, fox, wolf, deer, ox, horse, bear, tiger, hyena. From many of the bones of the gentler of these

animals being found in a broken state, it is supposed that the
cave was the haunt of hyenas and other predaceous animals, by
which the smaller ones had been consumed.

We come last to the *Modern* or *Superficial Formation*, of which
the best specimen is the great Bedford level, that spreads over the
lower lands of Norfolk, Cambridgeshire, and Lincolnshire, consisting of accumulations of silt, drifted matter, and bog-earth,
some of which began before the earliest periods of British history.
When these accumulations are removed by artificial means, we
find below sometimes shells of recent species, and the remains of
an old estuary, sometimes sand-banks, gravel beds, stumps of
trees, and masses of drifted wood. On this recent surface are
found skulls of a living species of European bear, skeletons of
the Arctic wolf, European beaver and wild boar, and numerous horns and bones of the roebuck and red deer, and of the
gigantic stag or Irish elk. They testify to a zoology on the verge
of that now prevailing or melting into it. In corresponding deposits of North America are found remains of the mammoth,
mastadon, buffalo, and other animals of extinct or living species.

Considering it best not to interrupt the description of the successive formations, this is almost the only allusion that has been
made to the fossils which constitute so important a part of geological science. It is now to be explained that from an early
period, that is, from the metamorphic deposit to the close of the
rock series, each formation is found to enclose remains of the organic beings, plants, and animals, which flourished upon earth
during the time they were forming; and these organisms, or such
parts of them as were of sufficient solidity, have been in many
instances preserved with the utmost fidelity, although for the
most part converted into the substance of the enclosing mineral.
The rocks may be thus said to form a kind of history of the organic departments of nature apparently from near their beginning
to the present time. It is upon the commencement and progress
of life under these circumstances that the author of the *Vestiges
of Creation* has put forth some of his most startling and contro
versial propositions; but before noticing them it will be useful to
prepare the way by shortly describing the gradations of organic
existences, following the same order as observed in the rock

series, by beginning with the lowest or humblest forms of organization.

The interior of the earth reveals wonders not less impressive
than those of the skies.   We have seen in the last section how
the crust of our globe is composed of successive layers or tiers of
strata, rising upward, terrace upon terrace, till we reach the present vegetable mould or superficial platform of animated existence.   In the aggregate these formations or systems, marking
the several epochs in nature's development, may extend to a
depth, as Dr. BUCKLAND conjectures, of ten or fifteen miles below the surface, and each may be considered a vast cemetery or
graveyard, entombing the remains of ages long anterior to human creation.   We, in fact, live upon a pile of worlds, and an-
ticipating the future from past records and from changes still
manifest from the shallowing soundings of neighbouring seas,
it is not improbable that the existing scene of bustle may have
heaped upon it as many superincumbent masses as the lowest
of the rocks enclosing the vestiges of life.

If not with a kind of awe, it must have certainly been with intense curiosity that the first investigators of fossilology looked
upon the earliest forms of animated being of which we have any
traces as existing upon this globe.   These first denizens, however, seem to have been of a simple structure and humble
order, not fit to play high class characters.   No land animals are
found among them, none which could breathe the atmosphere,
none but tenants of the water, and even animals so high in the
scale as fish were wanting.   In popular language, the earliest
fossils are corals and shellfish.

But to make the subject generally intelligible it will be necessary first to define the orders of the animal kingdom.
CUVIER was the first to give a philosophical view of the animal
world in reference to the plan on which each animal is con-
structed.   According to him there are four forms on which
animals have been modelled, and of which ulterior divisions are
only slight modifications founded on the development or addition

of some parts that do not produce any essential change of structure.

The four great branches of the animal world are the *vertebrata*, *mollusca*, *articulata*, and *radiata*. The *vertebrata* are those animals which (as man and other sucklers, birds and fishes) have a backbone and a skull with lateral appendages, within which the viscera are excluded, and to which the muscles are attached. The *mollusca* or soft animals have no bony skeleton; the muscles are attached to the skin, which often include stony plates called shells; such mollusca are shell-fish, others are cuttle-fish, and many pulpy sea animals. The *articulata* consist of crustacea (lobsters, &c.), insects, spiders, and annulos worms, which, like the other classes of this branch, consist of a head and a number of successive portions of the body jointed together, whence the name. Finally the *radiata* include the animals known under the name of zoophytes.

Now it is fossils of the *radiata* division of the animal kingdom that are found in the lowest stratified rocks, polypiaria and crinodia, the first including various forms of these extraordinary animals (corallines) which still abound in tropical seas, often obstructing the course of the mariner, and even laying the foundation of new continents. The crinoids are an early and simple form of the large family of star-fishes; the animal is little more than a stomach, surrounded by tentacula to provide itself with food, and mounted upon a many-jointed stalk, so as to resemble a flower upon its stem. Along with these in the slate system are a few lowly genera of crustacea, and of a higher class, the mollusca, and the existence of these imply the contemporary existence of certain humbler forms of life, vegetable and animal, for their subsistence, forming a scene approaching to what is found in seas of the present day, excepting that fishes, nor any higher vertebrata, as yet roamed the marine wilds.

The animal species of this era seem to have been few in number, and almost the whole had become extinct before the next group of strata had been formed. In the Silurian deposit the vestiges of life become more abundant, the number of species extended, and important additions made in the traces of sea plants and fishes. Remains of fishes have been detected in rocks immediately over the Aymestry limestone, being apparently the first examples of vertebrated animals which breathed upon our planet. (p. 64). The cephaloda, represented in our era by the nautilus and cuttle-fish, pertain to the Silurian formation, and are the most highly organised of the mollusca, possessing in some families an internal bony skeleton, together with a heart and a head with mandibles not unlike those of the parrot.

In the Old Red Sandstone the same marine specimens are continued with numerous additions. Several of the strata are crowded with remains of fish, showing that the seas in which these beds were deposited had swarmed with that class of inhabitants. The predominating kinds are of an inferior model to the two orders which afterwards came into existence, and still are the principal fishes of our seas; the former are covered with integuments of a considerably different character from the true scales covering the latter, and which orders, from their form of organization, are named stenoid and cycloid.

Up to the present we find proofs of the general uniformity of organic life over the surface of the earth at the time when each particular system of rocks was formed. The types of being formed in the old red as in preceding deposits, are identical in species with the remains that occur in the corresponding class of rocks in Brittany, the Hartz, Norway, Russia, and North America; attesting the similarity and almost universality, if not contemporary character, of terrestrial changes. A few other geological facts may be here mentioned for recollection, and which throw light on the marine animal and vegetable forms of this and preceding eras. First there was comparatively an absence of salt in the early ocean; and next the temperature of the earth is conjectured to have been higher, and perhaps almost uniform throughout. The higher temperature of the primeval times is attributed to the greater proximity or intensity of the globe's internal heat, and which, poured through cracks and fissures of the lately concreted crust, M. BRONGNIART supposes to have been sufficiently great to overpower the ordinary meteorological influences and spread a tropical climate all over its surface.

It must be further borne in mind that as yet no *land animals*

or *plants* existed, and for this presumable reason, that dry land
had not appeared. It is only in the next or carboniferous formation that evidence is traced of island or continent. As a consequence of this emergence there was fresh water ; for rain, instead
of returning to the sea, as formerly, was collected in channels
of the earth and became springs, rivers, and lakes. It was made
a receptacle for an advance in organism, and land plants became
a conspicuous part of the new creation.

According to the *Vestiges of Creation*, terrestrial botany began
with classes of comparatively simple forms and structure. In the
ranks of the vegetable kingdom the lowest place is taken by
plants of cellular tissue, and which have no flowers, as lichens,
mosses, fungi, ferns, and sea-weeds. Above these stand plants
with vascular tissue, bearing flowers, and of which there are two
subdivisions : first, plants having one seed-lobe, and in which
the new matter is added within, of which the cane and palm
are examples ; second, plants having two seed lobes, and in
which the new matter is added on the outside under the bark, of
which the pine, elm, oak, and all the British forest trees are examples. Now the author of the *Vestiges* states that two-thirds
of the plants of this era belong to the cellular kind, but to this one
of his ablest critics (*Edinburgh Review* for July) demurs, assert-
ing that the carboniferous epoch shows a gorgeous *flora*—that
the first fruits of vegetable nature were not rude, ill-fashioned
forms, but in magnificence and complexity of structure equal to
any living types, and that the forest approached the rank and
complicated display of a tropical jungle, where the prevalence of
great heat with great moisture, combined with the fact that the
atmosphere contained a greater proportion of the natural food of
plants, must undoubtedly have forcibly stimulated vegetation,
and in quantity and luxuriance of growth, if not fineness of organization, produced it in rich abundance. The earth, it is likely,
was one vast forest, which would perform a most important part
for the good of its future inhabitants, helping to purge the air of
its excess of carbonic acid, by which the earth's surface would be
prepared for its new occupants.

The animal remains of this era are not numerous in comparison with those that go before or follow. Contrary to what the

author of the *Vestiges* supposes (p. 111), insects were already
buzzing in the air; there were, however, no crawling reptiles on
the ground, and it is a doubtful point whether birds cheered the
ancient forests with their song. But fishes reached their most
perfect organic type. They were the lords of creation, and had
a structure in conformity with their high office. Since then the
class has increased in its species, but has degenerated to a less
noble type.

In the next formation, the New Red Sandstone, reptiles make
their appearance. They are considered next to fishes in the
zoological scale. So nearly are they sometimes connected, that
it is doubtful to which class they belong. Many reptiles arc also
amphibious, adapted either to water or land. The surface of
the globe abounded in large flat, muddy shores, and was suited
to the new order of visitants called into existence.

In the Oolite System, mostly consisting of calcareous beds, mam-
mals make their appearance. Some additions were made to the
reptile form. One animal (the behemite) appeared, but termi-
nated in the next era. In the following series of rocks mam-
mals increase in abundance. The advance in land animals
is less marked, but considerable in the tertiary strata. The tapir
forms a conspicuous type. One animal of the kind was eighteen
feet long, and had a couple of tusks turning down from the lower
jaw, by which it could attach itself, like the walrus, to a bank,
while its body floated in the water. Many animals of a former period disappear, and are replaced by others belonging to still exis-
tent families—elephant, hippopotamus, and rhinoceros—though
extinct as species. Some of these forms are startling from their
size. The great mastadon was a species of elephant living on
aquatic plants, and reaching the height of twelve feet. The
mammoth was another elephant, and supposed to have survived
till comparatively recent times. The megatherium is an incon-
gruity of nature, of gigantic proportions, yet ranking in a much
humbler order than the elephant, that of the edenta, to which
the sloth, ant-eater, and armadilla belong. The megatherium
had a skeleton of enormous solidity, with an armour-clad body,
and five toes, terminating in huge claws to grasp the branches on

which it fed.   Finally, beside the dog, cat, squirrel, and bear, we have offered to us, for the first time, oxen, deer, camel, and other specimens of the rumantia.   Traces of the quadrumane, or monkey, have been found in the older tertiaries of France, India, and England.   So that we may now be said to have arrived at the zoological forms not long antecedent to the appearance of the chief of all, bimana, or man, and shall here pause to consider the conclusions of the author of the *Vestiges of Creation* on the origin of the organic existences that have been successively exhibited.

It will be convenient, however, first to introduce a synoptic view of the evolutions of the earth as set forth in this and the preceding section.   For this purpose the author has introduced a parallel table, exhibiting on one side a scale of animal life beginning with the humblest and ascending to the highest species ; and on the other side the successive series of rock formations, in which their fossiliferous remains have been found up to the present superficial deposits of the globe.   Objections have been made to the correctness of the author's analogies, scale, and his classification of animals, the chief of which will be adverted to in the next section ; but the table is essential, as presenting at one view an outline of the hypothesis he has sought to establish.

SCALE OF ANIMAL KINGDOM.   ORDER OF ANIMALS IN

Invertebrata.

1 Infusoria	*Traces of Infusoria* (?)	.. ..
2 Polypi	Polypiaria	
5 Echinodermata..	Echinodermata	

Mollusca.
- 7 Brachiopoda
- 9 Pteropoda..
- 10 Gasteropoda
- 11 Cephalopoda

Articulata.
- 15—20 Crustacea
- 12—14 Annelides

Brachiopoda..	Crus-
Pteropoda	tacea
Gasteropoda..	Annel-
Cephalopoda..	ides.

Vertebrata.

	Remains of Fishes .. .. ..
32—36 Fishes..	Fishes of low type; heterocercal; allied to crustacea .. ..
	Sauroid Fishes .. ..
37 Batrachia (frogs, &c.)	Batrachia .. ..
39 Sauria (lizards, &c.)	Sauria .. ..
40 Chelonia (tortoises)..	Chelonia .. ..
41—46 Birds	*Footsteps of Birds* .. .. ..
47 Cetacea (dolphins, whales, &c.) ..	*Bones of a Cetaceous Animal* ..
	Bones of a Marsupial .. ..
48 Pachydermata (tapirs, &c.)	Pachydermata .. ..
49 Edentata (sloths)	Edentata .. ..
50 Rodentia (squirrels, hare, &c.) ..	Rodentia .. ..
51 Marsupialia (opossums, &c.)	Marsupialia .. ..
52 Ruminantia (oxen, stag, &c.)	Ruminantia .. ..
53 Amphibia (seals)	
54 Digitigrada (dog, cat, &c.)	Digitigrada .. ..
55 Plantigrada (bear, &c.)	Plantigrada .. ..
56 Insectivora (shrew, &c.)..	Insectivora .. ..
57 Cheiroptera (bats)	Cheiroptera .. ..
58 Quadrumana (apes)..	Quadrumana.. .. .. ..
29 Bimana (man)	Bimana.. .. ..

ASCENDING SERIES OF ROCKS.	FŒTAL HUMAN BRAIN RESEMBLES, IN
1 Gneiss and Mica Slate System	
2 Clay Slate System	1st month, typically, that of an avertebrated animal;
3 Silurian system	
4 Old Red Sandstone	2nd month, that of a fish;
5 Carboniferous formation	
6 New Red Sandstone	3rd month, that of a turtle; 4th month, that of a bird;
7 Oolite	
8 Chalk	
	5th month, that of a rodent;
	6th month, that of a ruminant;
9 Tertiary	7th month, that of a digitigrade animal;
	8th month, that of the quadrumana
10 Superficial deposits	9th month, attains full human character.

c 2

TRANSMUTATION OF SPECIES.

In the two last sections we have gone through the earth's geological history, first of the changes in its physical structure, next of the mutations in the organic forms that have, in serial order, appeared in the successive strata of its external envelope, from the period of that far distant crisis when it was a molten globe on which its primitive granitic covering was just beginning to concrete, in consequence of abating heat, until we have arrived at the first prognostic signs of approaching human existence.

The rock upon rock of vast thickness, by which the earth's crust, through countless ages, has been formed, unquestionably constitutes a most extraordinary phenomenon of physical creation, but hardly so marvellous and incomprehensible as the beginning, progress, and end of the divers orders of marine and terrestrial beings that filled each world of life.   It is to geologists, to PLAYFAIR, HUTTON, LYELL, BUCKLAND, SEDGWICK, OWEN, and other great names, native and foreign, to whom we are indebted for this singular revelation of Nature's works.   It is their unwearied research that has opened to us the surprising spectacle we have attempted briefly to describe of the diversified groups of species which have, in the course of the earth's history, succeeded each other at vast intervals of time; one set of animals and plants wholly or partly disappearing from the face of our planet, and others, which apparently did not before exist, becoming the only or predominant occupants of the globe.

Now the great question arises—whence, by what power, or by what law, were these reiterated transitions brought about? Were the organized species of one geological epoch, by some long-continued agency of natural causes, transmuted into other and succeeding species? or were there an extinction of species, and a replacement of them by others, through special and miraculous acts of creation? or, lastly, did species gradually degenerate and die out from the influence of the altered and unfavourable physical conditions in which they were placed, and be supplanted by immigrants of different species, and to which the new conditions were more congenial?

The last, we confess, is the view to which we are most inclined—first, because we think a transmutation of species, from a lower to a higher type, has not been satisfactorily proved; and second, because of the strong impression we entertain, that the universe, subject to certain cyclical and determinate mutations, was made complete at first, with self-subsisting provisions for its perpetual renewal and conservation. We shall advert to this matter hereafter; but at present it is the conclusions of the author of the *Vestiges* that claim consideration. He adopts the first interpretation of animal phenomena, namely, that there has been a transmutation of species, that the scale of creation has been gradually advancing in virtue of an inherent and organic law of development. Nature, he contends, began humbly; her first works were of simple form, which were gradually meliorated by circumstances favourable to improvement, and that everywhere animals and plants exhibit traces of a parallel advance of the physical conditions and the organic structure. The general principle, he inculcates, is, that each animal of a higher kind, in the progress of its embryo state, passes through states which are the final condition of the lower kind; that the higher kinds of animals came later, and were developed from the lower kinds, which came earlier in the series of rock formations, by new peculiar conditions operating upon the embryo, and carrying it to a higher stage. These conclusions the author maintains geology has established, and of the results thence derived he gives the subjoined recapitulation:—

"In pursuing the progress of the development of both plants and animals upon the globe, we have seen an advance in both cases, from simple to higher forms of organization. In the botanical department we have first sea, afterwards land plants; and amongst these the simpler (cellular and cryptogamic) before the more complex. In the department of zoology, we see, first, traces all but certain of infusoria [shelled animalculæ]; then polypiaria, crinoidea, and some humble forms of the articulata and mollusca; afterwards higher forms of the mollusca; and it appears that these existed for ages before there were any higher types of being. The first step forward gives fishes, the humblest class of the vertebrata; and, moreover, the earliest fishes partake of the character of the lower sub-kingdom, the articulata. Afterwards come land animals, of which the first are reptiles, universally allowed to be the type next in advance from fishes, and to be connected with there by the links of an insensible gradation. From reptiles we advance to birds, and thence to mammalia, which are commenced by marsupialia, acknowledgedly low forms in their class. That there is thus a progress of some kind, the most superficial glance at the geological history is sufficient to convince us."

Now this appears plausible and conclusive, but the correctness of the recapitulation here made, and its conformity to actual nature, have been sharply disputed. It may be true that sea plants came first, but of this there is no proof; and of land plants there is not a shadow of evidence that the simpler forms came into being before the more complex : the simple and complex forms are found together in the more ancient *flora*. It is true that we first see polypiaria, crinoidea, articulata, and mollusca, but not exactly in the order stated by the author. It is true that the next step gives us fishes, but it is not true that the earliest fishes link on to the lower sub-kingdom, the articulata. It is true that we afterwards find reptiles, but those which first appear belong to the highest order of the class, and show no links of an insensible gradation into fishes. In the tertiary deposit of the London clay the evidence of concatenation entirely fails. Among the millions of organic forms, from corals up to mammalia of the London and Paris basins, hardly a single secondary species is found. In the south of France it is said that two or three secondary species struggle into the tertiary strata; but they form a rare and evanescent exception to the general rule. Organic nature at this stage seems formed on a new pattern—plants as well as animals are changed. It might seem as if we had been transported to a new planet; for neither in the arrangement of the genera and the species, nor in their affinities with the types of a pre-existing world, is there any approach to a connected chain of organic development.

For some discrepancies the author endeavours to account, and it is fair to give his explanation :—

"Fossil history has no doubt still some obscure passages ; and these have been partially adverted to. Fuci, the earliest vegetable fossils as yet detected, are not, it has been remarked, the lowest forms of aquatic vegetation; neither are the plants of the coal-measures the very lowest, though they are a low form, of land vegetation. There is here in reality no difficulty of the least importance. The humblest forms of marine and land vegetation are of a consistence to forbid all expectation of their being preserved in rocks. Had we possessed, contemporaneously with the fuci of the Silurians, or the ferns of the carboniferous formation, fossils of higher forms respectively, *equally unsubstantial,* but which had survived all contingencies, then the absence of mean forms of similar consistency might have been a stumbling-block in our course ; but no such phenomena are presented. The blanks in the series are therefore no more than blanks; and when a candid mind further considers that the botanical fossils actually present are all in the order of their organic development, the whole phenomena appear exactly what might have been anticipated. It is also remarked, in objection, that the mollusca and articulata appear in the same group of rocks (the slate system) with polypiaria, crinoidea, and other specimens of the humblest sub-kingdom ; some of the mollusca, moreover, being cephalopods, which are the highest of their division in point of organization. Perhaps, in strict fact, the cephalopoda do not appear till a later time, that of the Silurian rocks. But even though the cephalopoda could be shewn as pervading all the lowest fossiliferous strata, what more would the fact denote than that, in the first seas capable of sustaining any kind of animal life, the creative energy advanced it, in the space of one formation, (no one can say how long a time time this might be,) to the highest forms possible in that element, excepting such as were of vertebrate structure. It may here be inquired if geologists are entitled to set so high a value as they do upon the point in the scale of organic life which is marked by the upper forms of the mollusca. It will afterwards be seen that this is a low point compared with the whole scale, if we are to take as a criterion that parity of development which has been observed in the embryo of one of the higher animals. *The human embryo passes through the whole space representing the invertebrate animals in the first month, a mere fraction of its course.* There is indeed a remarkably rapid change of forms in such an embryo at first: the rapidity, says Professor Owen, is ‘in proportion to the proximity of the ovum to the commencement of its development;’ and, conformable to this fact, we find the same zoologist stating that, in the lowest division of the animal kingdom, (the Acrita of his arrangement,) there is a much quicker advance of forms towards the next above it, than is to be seen in subsequent departments. There is, indeed, to the most ordinary observation, a rapidity and force in the productive powers of the lowest animals, which might well suggest an explanation of that rush of life which seems to be indicated in the slate and Silurian rocks. With regard to the so-called early occurence of fishes partaking of the saurian character, I would say that their occurrence a full formation after the earliest and simplest fishes, is, considering how little we know of the space of time represented by a formation, not early : their being later in any degree is the fact mainly important. The subsequent rise of new orders of fishes, fully piscine in character, may be explained by the supposition of their having been developed, as is most likely, from a different portion of the inferior sub-kingdom. In short, all the objections which have been made to the great fact of a general progress of organic development throughout the geological ages, will be found, on close examination, to refer merely to doubtful appearances of small moment, which vanish into nothing when rightly understood."

Upon some of the chief points here involved, it may be remarked that the most eminent physiologists are not agreed; they are not agreed that animals can be arranged in a series, passing from lower to higher; nor that animals of a higher kind in the embryo state pass through the successive stages of the lower kinds; the character of these stages, in the asserted doctrine, being taken from the brain and heart, and man being the highest point of the series. There are physiologists too who deny that the brain of the human embryo at any period, however early, resembles the brain of any mollusk or of any articulata. It never, they assert, passes through a stage comparable or analogous to a permanent condition of the same organ in any invertebrate animal; and in like manner the spinal cord in the human vertebræ at no period agrees with the corresponding part of the lower kind of animals. The moment it becomes visible in the human embryo, it is entirely dorsal in position; while in mollusks and articulatas a great part, or nearly the whole, is ventral. The same is true of the heart, or centre of the vascular system, which has always a different relative position in the great nervous centre in the human embryo from what it has in any articulate animal, and in most mollusks.

· A second position in the *Vestiges* appears not to have been established—namely, as to the uniform geological arrangement of different organic structures. It is not true that *only* the lowest forms of animal life are found in the lowest fossiliferous rocks, and that the more complicated structures are gradually and exclusively developed among the higher bands in what might be called a natural ascending scale. On the contrary, the predaceous cephalopods and the highly organized crustaceous are among the oldest fossils. Such appears to be the order of nature as evidenced by facts, and it must be admitted, however repugnant to preconceived notions or mere mortal conjectural amendments.

In the third place the evidence seems to preponderate in favour of *permanency of species*. There can be no doubt that both plants and animals may, by the influence of breeding, and of external agents operating upon their constitution, be greatly modified, so as to give rise to varieties and races different from what before existed. But there are limits to such modifications, as in the different kind and breed of dogs; and no organized beings can, by the mere working of natural causes, be made to pass from the type of one species to that of another. A wolf by domestication, for example, can never become a dog, nor the ourang-outang by the force of external circumstances be brought within the circle of the human species.

In this opinion Mr. LYELL, Dr. PRICHARD, and Mr. LAWRENCE, concur. The general conclusion at which they have arrived is, that there is a capacity in all species to accommodate themselves to a certain extent to a change of external circumstances; this extent varying greatly according to the species. There may thus be changes of appearance or structure, and some of these changes are transmissible to the offspring; but the mutations thus superinduced are governed by certain laws, and confined within certain limits. Indefinite divergence from the original type is not possible, and the extreme limit of possible variation may usually be reached in a short period of time; in short, Professor WHEWELL concludes (*Indications of Creation*, p. 56), *that every species has a real existence in nature*, and a transmutation from one to another does not exist. Thus for example, CUVIER remarks that, notwithstanding all the differences of age, appearance and habits, which we find in the dogs of various races and countries, and though we have (in the Egyptian mummies) skeletons of this animal as it existed 3,000 years ago, the relation of the bones to each other remains essentially the same; and with all the varieties of their shape and size, there are characters which resist all the influences, both of external nature, of human intercourse, and of time.

What varieties, again, in the forms of the different breeds of horses and horned cattle; racers, hunters, coach horses, dray horses, and ponies; short-horns and long-horns, Devons and Herefords, polled galloways and Shetlands; how unlike are the unimproved breeds of cattle as they existed a century ago before the march of agricultural improvement began, and how different were most of these as then existing in what may be called the normal state from the wild cattle produced in Chillington Park. It has been found, however, when external and artificial conditions are removed, and these different breeds are allowed to run wild, as in the Pampas and Australia, no matter what the diversity of size, shape, and colour of the domestic breeds, they reverted in their wild state, in these respects, to their primitive types.

So again with regard to cultivated vegetables and flowers. How different are the species of the red cabbage and the cauliflower; who would have expected them to be varieties of the wild *brassica oleracea?* Yet from that they have been derived by cultivation. They have, however, a tendency like animals to revert to the original type, or, in the gardener's phrase, to degenerate, which it requires the utmost care on his part to counteract. When left to a state of nature, they speedily lose their acquired forms, properties and character, and regain those of the original species.

If species be permanent—if no education or training can educe new kinds—if the higher classes of animals are not the results of meliorations of the lower—whence did they come? This question we are not bound to answer. It might be as reasonably asked, whence did the lower classes come? Geology, like other sciences, does not conduct us to the *beginning,* it only takes up creation at certain ulterior stages of development. The changes and construction of the globe may have been different in different parts; it has not been proved that geological revolutions have been either universal or contemporary. There may have been climates and regions adapted to the existence of the higher class of land animals, while contemporarily therewith other portions of the globe might be undergoing changes beneath the ocean. It is not improbable that the human species dwelt nearly stationary for ages on the old continents of Africa and Asia, while Europe and America were covered with water. Supposing these new continents formed, either by the gradual subsidence of the sea or the rising of its bed, successive inhabitants would follow in the order presented by existing organic remains. While covered by the sea, what now form Europe and America could only be peopled by marine animals; but as the land rose or the waters subsided into

.their ocean channels, and dry land appeared, reptiles and amphi-
bize might become the occupants; next, as the earth became
drier and more salubrious, the new continent would be resorted
to by terrestrial animals; in a still more advanced stage of puri-
fication and salubrity, man himself, as the lord of all the preceding classes of immigrants, would take possession, and as he
still continues the living occupant it is premature to look for his
petrifaction.

ORIGIN OF THE ANIMATED TRIBES.

Science has mastered many perplexities, but is almost power-
less as ever in generation. All that lives, and still more all that
moves, must have a pre-existing germ formed independently of
the created being, but which is essential to its existence, and
fixes the type of organization. The old adage—*omne animal
ab ovo*—may be taken as generally true. But though every animal has its primordial egg or germ, all germs are not identical.
In the beginning of life there are other organic elements besides
the ovum. Partly on direct proof and partly on good analogy, it
may be inferred that these differ in different species—that each in
the first stages of existence is bound by a different and immutable
mode of development—and, if so, there can be no embryotic
identity. " By no change of conditions," says Dr. CLARKE,
" can two ova of animals of the same species be developed into
different animal species; neither by any provision of identical
conditions can two ova of different species be developed into
animals of the same kind." If these views be right, and we believe them to be so, there cannot be a transmutation of species
under the influence of external circumstances.

Baffled in the effort either to create species or organically to
change them, attempts have been made to approach nearer to the
source of vitality, and explain the chemical, electric, or mechanical laws by which the vital principle is influenced. For this purpose various hypotheses have been put forth; one is the noted
conjecture of Lord MONBODDO, that man is only an advanced
development of the chimpanzee or ourang-outang. A second
explanation is that given by LAMARCK, who surmised, and with
much ingenuity attempted to prove, that one being advanced in
the course of generations into another, in consequence merely of

the experience of wants calling for the exercise of faculties in a particular direction, by which exercise new developments of organs took place, ending in variations sufficient to constitute new species. In this way the swiftness of the antelope, the claws and teeth of the lion, the trunk of the elephant, the long neck of the giraffe have been produced, it is supposed, by a certain plastic character in the construction of animals, operated upon for a long course of ages by the attempts which these animals make to attain objects which their previous organization did not place within their reach. This is what is meant by the hypothesis of *progressive tendencies*, and which requires for its validity not only the assumption of a mere capacity for change, but of active principles conducive to improvement and the attainment of higher powers and faculties. More recently St. Hilaire has published a paper in which he speaks of the immutability of species as a conviction that is on the decline, and that the age of Cuvier is on the close. Carried away by what Professor Phillips has called a poetical conjecture that cannot be proved, this writer propounded the speculation that the present crocodiles are really the offspring of crocodilian reptiles, the difference being merely the effect of physical conditions, especially operating during long geological periods upon one original race. The human species, he contends, are but an advanced development of the higher order of the monkey tribe, and that the negroes are degenerating towards that type again. According to him the sivatherium—a fossil animal that had been found in the Himalaya mountains—was the primeval type that time had fined down into the giraffe from long-continued feeding on the branches of trees. Dr. Falconer and Capt. Cautley, however, have shown that anatomical proofs are all against this inference, but if any doubt remained it must yield to the fact, that among the *fauna* of the Sewalik hills the sivatherium and the giraffe were contemporaries.

The author of the *Vestiges of Creation* has put forth an hypothesis founded on the preceding conjectures, but more compact and conclusive. He is, as we have seen, in favour of the progressive change of species, adopting the notion that men once had tails, and that the rudiments of this condal appendage are found in an undeveloped state in the *os coccygis* (p. 199.) His leading idea of the progress of organic life is that the " *simplest and most primitive type under a law to which that of like production is subordinate, gave birth to the type next above it; that this again produced the next higher, and so on to the very highest,* the stages of advance being in all cases very small—namely, from one species only to another; so that the phenomenon has always been of a modest and simple character." (p. 231.) The arguments by which the author endeavours to prove his hypothesis may be thus compressed.

According to him fœtal development is a science, illustrated by HUNTER's great collection of the Royal College of Surgeons, and established by the conclusions of ST. HILAIRE and TIEDMANN. Its primary positions are—1. That the embryos of all animals are not distinguishably different from each other; and, 2. That those of all animals pass through a series of phases of development, each of which is the type or analogue of the permanent configuration of tribes inferior to it in the scale. Higher the order of animals, the more numerous its stages of progress. Man himself is not exempt from this law. His first fœtal form is that which is permanent in the animalcule; it next passes through ulterior stages, resembling successively a fish, a reptile, a bird, and the lower mammalia before it attains its specific maturity. The period of gestation determines the species; protract it, and the species is advanced to a higher class. This might be done by the force of certain conditions operating upon the system of the mother. Give good conditions and the young she produces will improve in development; give bad conditions and it will recede. Cases of monstrous birth in the human species are appealed to, in which the most important organs are left imperfectly developed; the heart, for instance, having sometimes advanced no further than the three-chambered or reptile form, while there are instances of that organ being left in the two-chambered or fish-like form. These defects arise from a failure of the power of development in the mother, occasioned by misery or bad health, and they are but the converse of those conditions that carry on species to species. The *differences of sexes* is the result of fœtal progress only one degree less marked than that of a change of species. Sex is fully ascertained to be a matter of development. All beings are at one stage of the

embryotic progress *female*. A certain number of them are afterwards advanced to the more powerful sex. For proof of this,
the economy of boes is cited ; when they wish to raise a queen-
bee, or true female, they prepare for the larva a more commodi-
ous cell, and feed it with delicate food. But we shall here stop
to remark on the author's argument up to this point.

It is manifest, according to his hypothesis, that neither sex
nor species depend on the ancestral germ, but simply on physical
conditions and mechanical development. But eminent physiologists deny that the facts are such as he has stated ; they deny, as
we have stated in a former section, that the fœtal progress is such
as the *Vestges* represent them to be ; they deny that the human
embryo, for example, exhibits in successive stages the form of
fish, lizard, bird, beast : on the contrary, they contend that it is
only in the earliest period of the organic germ, when the manifestations are almost too obscure for microscopic sense, that any
resemblance exists ; that immediately the organic germ becomes
sensible to observation, sex and species are found to be fixed.
Take, for example, the vertebrata ; in these, by some mysterious
bond of union, the organic globules are seen to arrange themselves into two nearly parallel rows. We may then say that
the keel of the animal is laid down, and in it we have the first
rudiments of a backbone and a continuous spinal chord. But
during the progress and completion of this first organic process
no changes have been observed assimilating the nascent embryo
to any of the inferior animals. The next series of changes in
the germinal membrane are of two kinds—in one the nervous
system, the organs of motion, the intestinal canal, the heart and
blood-vessels are manifested ; the other set of changes, which
are subsequent, produce the perfection of the animal and de-
termine its sex. All these manifestations result from germinal
appendages that cannot be severed or changed without ruin to
the embryo, and the conditions essential to life as the structure
advances are due temperature, due nutriment of the nervous
organs, and due access to the atmospheric air. Without, therefore, pursuing further this part of the inquiry, we shall remark
that the question at issue between the *Vestiges* and its opponents
is one of facts—of conflicting evidence—to be tried by the jury
of the public, or rather by those who, from science or professional

pursuits, are competent to form an authoritative opinion. Our own conclusion is, that in face of the testimony adduced against it, the author's hypothesis is not yet established.

For proof that species do change, and that even new species have been actually and recently produced, the author has adduced statements certainly as questionable and little satisfactory as his representation of fœtal phenomena. We can only briefly enumerate them. First we are told that oats sown at midsummer, if kept cropped down, so as to be prevented shooting into ear, and then allowed to remain in the ground over winter, will spring up next year in the form of rye (p. 226). This need not be disputed about; the experiment can be easily tried; but if rye were the result, it would be no conclusive proof of a translation of species. Perhaps the oat-plants perished under the operation of repeated cuttings, and the rye seed was dormant in the earth and sprung up in its place; or, if not so, oats and rye may not be different species, only varieties of the same species. They are scarcely more dissimilar than the primrose, the cowslip, and the oxlip, which have all been raised from the seed of the same plant, and are now regarded by botanists as varieties instead of species.

When lime is laid on waste ground we are told that white clover will spring up spontaneously, and in situations where no clover-seed could have been left dormant in the soil (p. 182). But how is this to be proved? It is certain that seeds will remain dormant in the soil for centuries, and then spring up the first year the soil is turned up by the plough. Some seeds have retained their vitality for thousands of years in the old tombs of Egypt; they have been repeatedly brought to England, sown, and produced good wheat.

We are next told that wild pigs never have the measles, they are produced by a *hyatid* and the result of domestication; that a *tinea* is found in dressed wool that does not exist in its unwashed state; that a certain insect disdains all food but chocolate, and that the larva of *oinopota cellaris* only lives in wine and beer. All these are articles manufactured by man, and are adduced as proofs of animal life, independent of any primordial egg. The entoza are dwelt upon; they are creatures living in the interior of other animals, of which the tape-worm that infests the human body is a melancholy instance. In these illustrations we think the author has somewhat of reason, for we feel convinced that there is such a thing as spontaneous generation from the inorganic substances, wisely provided for clearing the earth of noxious effluvia and putrid matter, and converting them into new elements conducive to health and life. We believe in this source of vitality from its wisdom and necessity, its necessity and wisdom, in our estimate, being strong presumptive proofs of its existence in harmony with the general forecast and economy of nature. Of the self-originating spring of life, some of the examples adduced by the author are proofs, and of which we have familiar illustrations in cheese-mites, maggots in carrion, and the green fly that breeds so profusely in weak and decaying vegetation; in all which by some inscrutable law the organic germ, without any antecedent, appears to evolve from the dead or putrifying mass, for its riddance and transmutation.

Conceding, however, thus far to the author, we are not prepared to admit that the creative powers of Messrs. CROSSE and WEEKES has been established. These gentlemen are said (p. 190) to have introduced a stranger in the animal kingdom, a species of acarus or mite amidst a solution of silica submitted to the electric current. The insects produced by the action of a galvanic battery continued for eleven months are represented as minute and semi-transparent, and furnished with long bristles. One of the creatures resulting from this elaborate term of gestation was observed in the very act of emerging, in its first-born nudity, and sought concealment in a corner of the apparatus. Some of them were observed to go back into the parent fluid and occasionally they devoured each other; and soon after they were called to life, they were disposed to multiply their species in the common way! So much for the experiment; against its verity it is alleged, first, that the Acarus Crossii are not a new species, or if new, that neither Mr. CROSSE nor Mr. WEEKES, who repeated Mr. CROSSE's experiment, produced them, but only aided by the voltaic battery the development of the insects from their eggs. Such a mode of generation is contrary to all human experience, and can only be believed in on the strongest corroborative proof.

Neither by chemistry nor galvanism can man, we apprehend,

be more than instrumental and co-operative, not originally and independently creative. In almost every form of life, whether animal or vegetable, art can multiply varieties,—can train, direct —but cannot form new species. This is the mockery of science. With all its invention and resource, it cannot produce organic originals. It can rear a crab-apple into a golden-pippin, or wild sea-weed into a luxuriant cabbage; it can raise infinite varieties of roses, tulips, and pansies, but can create no new plant, fruit, or flower. Man can make a steam-engine, or a watch, but he cannot make a fly, a midge, or blade of grass. He is an ingenious compiler, but not a creator; and his powers of manufacture and conversion are restricted within narrow boundaries. He cannot wander far in the indulgence of his fancies without being recalled, and compelled to return to the first models set by the Great Architect. The further he strays from primitive types in the effort to improve, by crossing, cutting, and grafting, and proportionably less becomes the procreative force. Hybrids are notoriously sterile. Garden fruit is not permanent, and requires to be renewed from seed. The law seems universal in plants and animals, that the vital energy or germ is less forcible and prolific in the pampered and artificial, than in the natural and wild races.

HYPOTHESIS OF THE VITAL PRINCIPLE.

It is ascertained that the basis of all vegetable and animal substances consists in nucleated cells—that is, cells having granules within them. Nutriment is converted into these before being assimilated by the system. It has likewise been noted that the globules of the blood are reproduced by the expansion of contained granules; "they are, in short," says the *Vestiges,* "*distinct organisms multiplied by the same fissiporous generation.* So that all animated nature may be said to be based on this mode of origin; *the fundamental form of organic being is a globule, having a new globule forming within itself,* by which it is in time discharged, and which is again followed by another and another, in endless succession. It is of course obvious, that if these globules could be produced by any process from inorganic elements, we should be entitled to say that the fact of a transit from the inorganic to the organic had been witnessed." (p. 176.)

D

"Globules," the author continues, "can be produced in albumen by electricity. If, therefore, these globules be identical with the cells which are now held to be reproductive, it *might* be said that the production of albumen by artificial means is the only step in the process wanting. This has not yet been effected." (p. 177.)

These are the advances towards generation by chemistry and electricity. The process, however, according to this detail, appears still far from complete. Albumen is to be produced " by artificial means ;" and even then we should doubt entire success. Chemists have long commanded the power to resolve the seeds of animal and vegetable life into their elements ; they have analysed them, and shown the exact weight and proportion of each constituent ; but they never could put them together again, or, by any similar compound produce the primordial egg or organic germ, from which a living being would arise. A connecting link —a vital spark, or animating soul—is always wanting to complete the existence of the Prometheus of the laboratory. Mark, too, the "*if*," and the "*might*," in this most lame and impotent hypothesis :—" *If*, therefore, these globules be identical with the cells which are held to be reproductive, it *might* be said," &c. Globules can be easily produced ; the passage of the electric fluid through water will produce aerial globules in rapid and expansive movement ; boys can produce them with suds and a tobacco-pipe in rapid succession, each, for aught we know, containing a "granule" that multiplies by "fissiporous generation." But these are not organic globules, and the author has committed the great perversion in language or logic of confounding the organic globule of life with the inorganic globule of a chemist. His theory is more fanciful than that of LAMARCK, from whom it is derived, and who had, at least, his *petit corps gelatineux* to begin with—to commence weaving organic tissue from—but our author's organic globule is not so substantive a conception ; and as he does not pretend to be able to produce even this by physical means, he has not made a single step in generation.

This we consider the least satisfactory and successful portion of the author's work. It assigns no intelligible cause for the origin of life—it only *begs the question*, by the substitution of one mystery for another. His law of DEVELOPMENT is of the same description,—without sense or significancy, unsupported by appitiable facts, and is not so comprehensible a cause of vital changes as LAMARCK's assigned progressive tendencies of animals to master the appliances essential to their wants.

ANIMAL AFFINITIES, INSTINCT, AND REASON.

The scheme of the *Vestiges* is uniformly and consistently worked out; all phenomena are resolved into gravitation and development—the first as the law of inorganic, the latter of organic matter. By the last, however, no new principle is revealed, only a new phrase devised, by the amplified application of which the author's entire system may be said to be *begged* rather than proved; since development is used in a sense implying an indefinite power of animate and inanimate creation; so that at last we make no new discovery, only grasp a new nomenclature.

But the author is always interesting, either by the novel display of facts or the ingenious concatenation of plausibilities. Consistently with his fundamental notion of animal transmutation, he tries to prove a family likeness or affinity from the humblest to the highest species. In this way he seeks to explain the marvel with respect to the huge bulk of many of the tertiary mammalia—the mammoth, mastadon, and megatherium; they were in immediate descent from the cetacea, or whale and dolphin tribe. (p. 267.) Again, human reason is considered no exclusive gift; it exists subordinately in the instinct of brutes, and is alleged to be nothing more than a mode of operation peculiar to the faculties in a humble state of endowment, or early stage of development. CUVIER and NEWTON are only intellectual expansions of a clown; and this notion is extended to moral obliquities, the wicked man being characterised as one "whose highest moral feelings are rudimental." (p. 358.) From a like principle the writer concurs with Dr. PRICHARD, hat mankind may have had a common origin; that there exists no diversities of colour or osseous structure not referable to climatable or other plastic agencies influencing the development of the different races, commencing with the lowest, or Negro tribe, and ascending upward through the intermediate aboriginal American, Mongolian, and Malay, to the last and most perfect stage of the Caucasian type.

Into the verity of these conclusions we are not called upon to enter ; they have been long in controversy, involve a great array of facts and inductive inferences, and we have only referred to them as corollaries or collaterals of the author's hypothetical fabric.

RELIGIOUS AND MORAL TENDENCIES.

We have no charge of impiety to bring against the *Vestiges*. Final causes, or to express ourselves more intelligibly, a *purpose* in creation, is nowhere impugned. The Deity is not degraded by impersonification in the form and frailties of mortality, but everywhere the author reverently bows to that august and unsearchable name, acknowledges the grand and benevolent design—the admirable adaptation of every created thing to its end and place, and finally concludes in a strain of grateful and exulting Optimism, that we confess we have not fully arrived at —namely, that everything "is very good." (p. 387.) From this impression we have only one constructive drawback to notice in the author's mechanical but fanciful constitution of the universe, by which a special Providence in the government of the world seems to be dispensed with, and the Almighty is placed in the sinecure position of the Grand Elector of the Abbé Sieyes, with nothing to do. But no divine attribute is abscinded—no glory of Omnipotence dimmed—whether it pleases him to rule by direct interpositions of power, or his own pre-ordained eternal laws.

Still less can we detect in the speculative inquiries of the *Vestiges* conclusions hostile to the moral and social interests of the community. Men are formed to be what they are ; vice and crime are the fruits of malorganization, and malorganization is the result of the unfavourable conditions in which the subject of it has been placed, prior or subsequent to birth. These are the author's leading metaphysical inculcations. They impose grave duties upon individuals and upon society, rightly understood and applied, but we cannot discern a hurtful tendency in them. They are useful knowledge, knowledge that it would be well for parents and rulers to master, by showing the importance of education, of favourable circumstances, and of good moral and physical training, for rearing happy, well-ordered, and virtuous members of the community. Supreme in intelligence, man, we firmly believe, is not less supremely blessed in the means of felicity, provided his real nature and position in the scheme of creation were understood, recognised, and carried out. He has his place, his office, and his destiny; he is no enigma but as an individual; "in the mass," as the author emphatically remarks, "he is a mathematical problem." His conduct is uniform and consistent; the result of known and ascertainable causes—causes calculable and predicable in their consequences, as the statistics of crime have incontestibly established.

GENERAL CONCLUSIONS ON THE VESTIGES.

The heavens are wonderful, and the earth is wonderful, and man, who, by force of intellect, has sought to comprehend the immensity of one and unravel the formation of the other, is hardly less wonderful than either. Still the great mystery remains unriddled; our researches have brought us no nearer the beginning, and the first cause of all continues unapproachable and undefinable as ever. Instead of explaining physical creation, we begin with it; we take the existence of matter for granted, and its attributes for granted, and forthwith begin to fabricate a universe, without first ascertaining whence was matter, or whence the laws by which it is impressed, and has been governed in its evolutions.

Nature's greatest phenomena are the celestial spaces and the bodies that fill them; our own planet and its living occupants. Upon each of these, their commencement and subsequent vicissitudes, the *Vestiges of Creation* have propounded an hypothesis, but one mystery is only sought to be explained by another still more mysterious. For the fiat of a Creator chemical affinities and mechanical laws have been substituted, but aided by these the author has failed to produce a world such as we find it. Hence we are again driven upon the old tradition, the old sacred authority, that the world was created out of nothing; and this is as easy to comprehend as the solution of the *Vestiges*, that it sprang from that which is certainly next to nothing—a heated fog or universal fire-mist.

When the author deals with the facts of science he interests and instructs, but when he speculates he only amuses or perphazes, without advancing knowledge. His terse and luminous description of the astral firmament deeply impresses with the might and the magnitude of the vast design; but when he attempts to account for the elimination of suns and worlds, their formation and arrangement, we are struck by the puerile folly of his conjectural presumptions.

Descending from this august and glittering canopy to our own planet, we are not less astonished by the exhibition of the extraordinary revolutions it has undergone. Geology is the true historian of the earth. Conducted by the lights it affords, we see an eternity of ages has rolled before us; we discover a series of worlds rising through the depths of ocean from the central sphere of heat, amidst boiling floods and volcanic fires, each new platform of existence, that countless periods of time had been requisite to form, peopled with its own congenial forms of organic life, mostly commencing with the simpler, and ascending by almost imperceptible gradations to the higher and more complex structures of being. We are struck by the correspondence, by the *pari passu* development and formation of the earth's crust and organic existences, and we are apt hastily to conclude that a relation has subsisted between them, that contemporary changes have been cause and effect, and that the improvement of the earth produced the correlative improvement in animals and plants.

This forms the author's second questionable hypothesis; it is plausible, but false—repugnant to fact and correct observation. We have no credible evidence that species have changed, or are changeable by the utmost efforts of art or favouring conditions; all we can effect is to improve them within definite limits, but not alter their characteristic types; and we have certain proof that neither man nor the animal nearly next to him in organization, has changed either in habits, disposition, form, or essential structure during the last 3,000 years. Resemblance is no proof of identity; and hence, though species run into each other by almost inappreciable shades of difference, it is no proof that they are derivative, or other than isolated and self-dependent creations. That they are such, and shall continue such, seems a fixed canon of Nature, who, apparently, has prescribed to each its circle of amendment and range, that like shall beget like—that nought organic shall exist without ancestral germ—and that the variety of species which constitutes the beauty and order of nature shall by no chance, contrivance, or mingling of races, be confounded.

Geological facts are in favour of this conclusion. They attest the appearance of new species, not their improvement. In each species a gradation of improvement, approximating from a lower to the next higher organism, is not perceptible; but each seems to have been made perfect at first, and most suited to the co-existent state of the earth. The earliest reptiles were not reptiles of inferior structure; nor the earliest fishes, birds, or beasts. They were adapted, as we now find them, to their precise sphere of existence, without progressive aptitude, preparatory to a higher and translated condition of being. Geology rather points to the extinction and degeneracy of species than their improvement; and the fossils of the old red sandstone, and of the carboniferous formation, attest a loftier and more magnificent creation of both marine and land products than any now subsisting.

For these and other reasons before adduced, we dismiss the hypothesis of animal transmutation as unproved and untenable. It pleases and satisfies superficial views, but confronted with the facts of nature, it vanishes like a baseless vision. Man is sui generis, sole and exclusive in organization, without pre-existing type or affinity to other species; and his alleged recent metamorphosis from a monkey, and his first and far more distant one from a snail or a tadpole, are paradoxes only worthy of idle debating clubs.

Having attempted to unfold the progression of species by his law of development, the author next essays to explain the commencement of the vital principle itself. But here, too, he must have a beginning, and his "organic globule" answers a similar purpose, in deducing the mystery of life, as his nuclei in the "nebular hypothesis." In both the perplexity and real difficulty is not solved or mastered, but evaded. But we have already remarked on the point, and shall only observe that when the author can elicit *thought* from inorganic matter, either by chemistry or galvanism, we shall think he has made a step in creation. Until then he does not advance, only deceives himself and readers by verbal subtleties and baseless suppositions.

Apart from its hypotheses, the *Vestiges* form a valuable and interesting work. It is the most complete, elaborate, and—with all its faults of detail, logic, and inference—the most scientific expositor of universal nature yet offered to the world But its hypotheses are unwarranted, not inductively derived, and can have no hold on men of science, supported as they mostly are by fanciful analogies, facts misunderstood or misstated, and illustrations selected without discrimination or applicability. Theories do sometimes conduce to the discovery of truth, but are often obstructive; occupy the mind, like theological controversy, without advancing science; and are viewed with the same aversion by the philosopher that the political abstractions tendered to the multitude by the demagogue are viewed by the patriotic legislator.

The work, however, will live, and deserves to live. The temple of nature has been looked into, not profoundly, perhaps, nor always successfully; but in a fearless spirit, and with a highly-accomplished mind. Had the divine Cosmos been more fully dwelt upon and depicted—had the harmony, beauty, and beneficence of creation been more fully and exclusively displayed—we should have been more gratified; but we are thankful, in the main, for what we have received. An impulse has been given to popular inquiry, and a vast field for discussion opened, from which we can prospectively discern neither less love for man, nor reverence for God.

Who the author is we have no certain knowledge. It is not, we suspect, Lord KING, nor Lord THURLOW, nor Lady BYRON; but it may be the author of the *Essay on the Formation of Opinions*, and of the *Principle of Representation*. Mr. BAILEY, of Sheffield, though little known, possesses the fine reasoning powers, intellectual grasp, independence of research, abstract analysis, and attic style, that would qualify him to produce the *Vestiges of Creation*, though we never heard that he is a great natural philosopher. But, as just hinted, deep science is not evinced by the *Vestiges*, only an able, systematic, and tasteful arrangement of its distant and recent advances.

"EXPLANATIONS:"

A SEQUEL TO THE

"VESTIGES OF THE NATURAL HISTORY OF CREATION."

(From the ATLAS of December 20, 1845.)

So many strong objections had been arrayed against the *Vestiges of Creation*, that the author was called upon to elucidate and reinforce his argument, or abandon the ground he had taken up. The more candid and equitable of his judges—those who were disposed to try him upon the merits, and independently test the claims of his inquiry, as in fairness it ought to be, as strictly a scientific speculation, regardless of any constructive bearings it might have on current opinions or prejudices—could not arrive at any more favourable conclusion than that he had failed to establish his hypotheses. Indeed this was the only verdict that could be safely delivered in. The impugners of the work were in the same helpless predicament as its author, who had, however, more venturously presumed to unravel unsearchable mysteries, concerning which, in the existing state of science, men can only conjecture, wonder, and adore, utterly unable to affirm or deny aught respecting them. What, for instance, with the remotest semblance of certainty, can be predicated of the stellar orbs? Is it not idle almost to speculate on the impenetrable secret of their origin when their very existence is undefinable—when their end, their glittering discs, and all but immeasurable distances are wholly unapproachable? Nor hardly less beyond our grasp is the commencement of organic existences. We do pride ourselves on recent advances to the sources of

entity; we tear up the dead, we torture the living, and sedulously
chronicle every beat of the heart and vibration of the brain to
slake an insatiable curiosity, yet how unsatisfactory our reach
towards the hidden springs of life—how limited our attainments,
when the creation of a single blade of grass, the humblest worm,
a poor beetle, or gadfly, would baffle the utmost structural skill
of the greatest philosopher! Into the fathomless depths of our
own globe we have also essayed to penetrate. Poor beings! of
three score and ten, whose utmost historical span extends only
to some thousands of years, have sought to trammel up the serene
vicissitudes of millions of ages anterior to their own existence!
Does not this savour of a vain research, or of a laudable thirst
for knowledge?

Over all these dark and solemn inscrutabilities, however, the
Vestiges undertook to throw a glare of light, to reveal their beginning, progression, order, relations, and law of development. Although daring in aim, the attempt was not to be wholly deprecated.
While religious freedom had been secured, philosophy had become
timid, official, and timeserving; retentive as FONTENELLE of
the truths within its grasp, and fearful to give utterance to aught
that might disturb the stillness of the temple, the lecture-room,
or fashionable auditory. Modern teachers had been used so
long to the Baconian go-cart, that they had become as apprehen-
sive of losing the inductive clue as the PALINURUSES of old of
the sight of the directing shore. But the time had arrived when
it seemed expedient to relax the strictness of the investigative
rule, and afford scope for a more systematic, if not speculative
research. Science had made great acquisitions, and it seemed
desirable, if only for experiment sake, to see what kind of
FRANKENSTEIN would result from the architectural union of her
scattered limbs. This formed the scope of the *Vestiges of Creation*; novelties were not propounded, only a portentous skeleton
raised from the truths physical astronomy, geology, chemistry,
physiology, and natural history had established. Does the
author recoil from his work? No; these *Explanations* attest
that he is steadfast in the worship of the idol of his brain.
He retracts nothing, he re-asserts, elucidates, and often dexte-
rously turns the weapons of the most formidable and orthodox of
his adversaries against them, by showing from their writings that

they had, in detail at least, acquiesced in the truths that they now, in a generalised form, seek to controvert and repudiate. So much adroitness and pertinacity in the author can hardly fail to provoke resistance, if not asperity, despite of the imperturbable temper in which he maintains the combat. The learned have been disturbed in their daily routine, by the discharge from an unknown hand, of a massive pyrites, that has diffused as much consternation among the herd of modish elocutionists, college tutors, and chimpanzee professors, as Jove's ligneous projectile among the lieges of the standing pool. For this commotion we have, on a former occasion, conceded that there existed valid reasons, and we hasten to see the way in which they have been met in the rejoinder before us; contenting ourselves, as we needs must, by briefly noticing some of the salient points of the controversy.

First of the Nebular Hypothesis. The chief objection to this theory is, that the existence of nebulous matter in the heavens is disproved by the discoveries made by the telescope of the Earl of Rosse. By the reach of this wondrous tube, masses of light, rendered apparently nebulous by their vast distance, have been resolved into clusters of stars, and thence the assumption seemed unwarrantable that any luminous matter, different from the solid bodies composing planetary systems existed in the heavenly spaces. But to this the author replies, that there are two classes of nebulæ—one resolvable into constellations—another comparatively near, that remains unaffected by telescopic power, and that until this last description can be separated, the nebular hypothesis is not disproved. It is thus brought to an issue of facts, both as to the existence of nebulæ of this latter kind, and the optical power to resolve them into distinct stars.

But the author can hardly claim this negative success in grappling with a second objection—namely, his assumed origin of *rotatory motion.* According to him, a confluence of atoms round a spherical centre of attraction, would cause the agglomerated mass to revolve upon its axis in the manner of our earth. This was denied by everybody the least acquainted with the laws of motion; and thus did one of his imaginary solutions of a great phenomenon of the universe fall dead to the ground. This he now seems to concede, but in a sentence unintelligible to us, in which an undoubted physical law is spoken of as only an *abstract truth* (p. 20). He obviously still clings to his first mistaken inference, and calls to his aid Professor NICHOL, whom he has also pressed into his service to help him over the last-mentioned difficulty by the Professor's affirmation of a diversity of nebulous clusters. But the Professor does not commit himself to the extent of the author; his aqueous whirlpool is cited from HERSCHEL, only in illustration, and correctly said to be produced by the unequal force of convergence of a fluid to a common centre. But the author's nuclei, disposed in his notable "fire-mist," did not act with unequal force on the ambient vapours, and whose central convergence in consequence, would not produce rotation or motion of any kind. This was the real matter in question, the author was taken up on his own premises, and the results he assumed to follow from them proved to be inconsistent with the unquestionable laws of gravitating matter.

He has gone over the geological portion of his subject with much care, but if competent, it would be impossible within our narrow limits to accompany him; nor could the discussion be made either, interesting or intelligible except to the scientific, who have devoted attention to an extremely curious, but still obscure and unsettled field of investigation. He has elaborately cleared up many points, and successfully, we think, answered some weighty objections, but we are not yet converts to his theory of organic development. One passage we shall extract; after adverting to the facts established by powerful evidence, that during the long term of the earth's existence, strata of various thickness were deposited in seas composed of matter worn away from the previous rocks; that these strata by volcanic agency were raised into continents, or projected into mountain chains, and that sea and land have been constantly interchanging conditions. He continues:—

"The remains and traces of plants and animals found in the succession of strata show that, while these operations were going on, the earth gradually became the theatre of organic being, simple forms appearing first, and more complicated afterwards. *A time when there was no life* is first seen. We then *see life begin, and go on;* but whole ages elapsed before man came to crown the work of nature. This is a wonderful revelation to have come upon the men of our time,

and one which the philosophers of the days of Newton could never
have expected to be vouchsafed. The great fact established by it is,
that the organic creation, as we now see it, was not placed upon the
earth at once; it observed a PROGRESS. Now we can *imagine* the
Deity calling a young plant or animal into existence instantaneously;
but we see that he does not usually do so. The young plant and also
the young animal go through a series of conditions, advancing them
from a mere germ to the fully developed repetition of the respective
parental forms. So, also, we can *imagine* Divine power evoking a
whole creation into being by one word; but we find that such had not
been his mode of working in that instance, for geology fully proves that
organic creation passed through a series of stages before the highest
vegetable and animal forms appeared. Here we have the first hint of
organic creation having arisen in the manner of natural order. The
analogy does not prove identity of causes, but it surely points very
broadly to natural order or law having been the mode of procedure in
both instances."

To the allusion in the last sentence there can be no demur;
that there is "natural order or law" in creation who will con-
test? But it is the author's law and the author's order that are
in dispute—his transmutation of species, the higher classes
emerging from and partly annihilating the lower, under meliorated conditions of being. That the simpler form of organic life
should first appear; that remains of invertebrated animals should
be first found; then, with these, fish, being the lowest of the
vertebrated; next, reptiles and birds, which occupy higher
grades; and finally, along with the rest, mammifers, the highest
of all—all this appears natural enough. *How could it be otherwise?* When the earth was a slimy bed, what but the lowest
forms of life—the molluscs, and other soft animals, without bony
structure—could possibly live in or occupy it? During the carboniferous era, when the earth was enveloped in an atmosphere
of hydrogen, vegetation might thrive; but man, and animals
like him, dependent on vital air, could not exist; nor are remains of them found in this epoch of the globe's vicissitudes.
All this is comprehensible. But the perplexing inquiry is, whence
did the successive grades of animals emerge? That they could
not contemporaneously exist; when the whole earth was a shore-
less sea, and that animals could not live is certain; but were they
created in succession by the Divine fiat, or did they emerge, as

our author supposes and elaborately tries to prove, from the
humblest primitive forms, by an inscrutable law of progression—
evidenced, he contends, by geological facts—though by some his
facts are disputed—and certainly not confirmed by any animal
changes observable within the limits of human experience?

There is another alternative offers, which would dispense both
with the author's hypothesis and the need of successive organic
creations by a special Providence. Is it a geological fact, since
life began, that the earth has *simultaneously* undergone throughout its entire surface the revolutions assigned to it? May it not
always, from that period, have consisted, as it now does, of
water and dry land, alternately changing their sites, but always
apart, and allowing of the contemporary existence on some portion of its surface of all the varieties of tribes ever found upon it?
The fossiliferous rocks that formed the primeval sea-beds could
only be deposited by the abrasion from the anterior and higher
rocks. It has always appeared to us that this conjecture is
worthy of consideration, and, if found tenable, would reconcile
many perplexities.

Upon subjects so obscure, and to which the human intellect
has been only recently directed, it is not surprising that men of
science have not arrived at uniformity of conclusion. Unable to
reconcile phenomena with positive knowledge, there are names
of no mean repute who would reserve certain domains of creation
as the fields of special interventions. To this class DR. WHE-
WELL appears to belong, who assumes that "events not included
in the *course of nature* have formerly taken place." In the
same way Professor SEDGWICK, to account for the appearance of
certain animals, says, "They were not called into being by any
law of nature, but by a power above nature." He adds, "they
were created by the hand of GOD, and adapted to the conditions
of the period." To this the author of the *Vestiges* assents, with
the explanation (p. 134) that their existence was not the result
of a "special exertion of power to meet special conditions," but
of an antecedent and primitive law of development suited to the
new exigencies, and emanating from the Creator. This, he
contends, does not lower our estimate of the Divine character;
and, in proof, cites DR. DODDRIDGE, who cannot be suspected of
irreverence. "When we assert," says the pious and amiable

author, "a perpetual Divine agency, we readily acknowledge that matters are so contrived as not to need a Divine interposition in a different manner from that in which it had been constantly exerted. And it must be evident that an unremitting energy, displayed in such circumstances, *greatly exalts our idea of God, instead of depressing it ;* and, therefore, by the way, is so much more likely to be true." Against constructive inferences it is urged, in the *Explanations*—

"As to results which may flow from any particular view which reason may show as the best supported, I most firmly protest against any assumed title in an opponent to pronounce what these are. The first object is to ascertain truth. No truth can be derogatory to the presumed fountain of all truth. The derogation must lie in the erroneous construction which a weak human creature puts upon the truth. And practically it is the true infidel state of mind which prompts apprehension regarding any fact of nature, or any conclusion of sound argument."

The writer then quotes Sir JOHN HERSCHELL as having some years ago announced views strictly conformable to those subsequently taken of organic creation in the *Vestiges* :—

" ' For my part,' says Sir John, 'I cannot but think it an inadequate conception of the Creator, to assume it as granted that his combinations are exhausted upon any one of the theatres of their former exercise, though, in this, as in all his other works, we are led, by *all analogy*, to suppose that he operates through a series of intermediate causes, and that, in consequence, *the origination of fresh species, could it ever come under our cognisance, would be found to be a natural, in contradistinction to a miraculous process,*—although we perceive no indications of any process actually in progress which is likely to issue in such a result. In his address to the British Association at Cambridge, (1845), he said with respect to the author's hypothsis of the first step of organic creation—' The transition from an inanimate crystal to a globule capable of such endless organic and intellectual development, is as great a step—as unexplained a one—as unintelligible to us—and in any sense of the word as *miraculous*, as the immediate creation and introduction upon earth, of every species and every individual would be!' "

The Rev. Dr. PYE SMITH is next adduced :—

" 'Our most deeply investigated views of the Divine Government,' says he, 'lead to the conviction that it is exercised in the way of *order*, or what we usually call *law*. God reigns according to immutable principles, that is *by law*, in *every part of his kingdom—the mechanical, the intellectual, and the moral ;* and it appears to be most clearly a position arising out of that fact, that *a comprehensive germ which shall necessarily evolve all future developments*, down to the minutest atomic movements, is a more suitable attribution to the Deity, than the idea of a necessity for irregular interferences.' "

Lastly, the reviewer of the *Vestiges* in *Blackwood's Magazine*, who is understood to be a naturalist of distinguished ability, expresses himself in an equally decided manner :—

" To reduce to a system the acts of creation, or the development of the several forms of animal life, no more impeaches the authorship of creation, than to trace the laws by which the world is upheld, and its phenomena perpetually renewed. The presumption naturally rises in the mind, that the same Great Being would adopt the same mode of action in both cases....To a mind accustomed, as is every educated mind, to regard the operations of Deity as essentially differing from the limited, sudden, evanescent impulses of a human agent, it is distressing to be compelled to picture to itself, the power of God as put forth *in any other manner than in those slow, mysterious, universal laws, which have so plainly an eternity to work in ;* it pains the imagination to be obliged to assimilate those operations, for a moment, to the brief energy of a human will, or the manipulations of a human hand........ No, there is nothing atheistic, nothing irreligious, in the attempt to conceive creation, as well as reproduction, carried on by universal laws."

We have dwelt so much upon this matter because it is one in which popular feelings are likely to be most deeply interested. We shall give the author, too, the benefit of his *Explanations* on another point, elucidating his former statement of the transmutation of a crop of oats into a crop of rye :—

" ' At the request,' says Dr. Lindley, ' of the Marquis of Bristol, the Reverend Lord Arthur Hervey, in the year 1843, sowed a handful of oats, treated them in the manner recommended, by continually stopping the flowering stems, and the produce, in 1844, has been for the most part ears of a very slender barley, having much the appearance of rye, with a little wheat, and some oats; samples of which are, by the favour of Lord Bristol, now before us.' The learned writer then adverts to the 'extraordinary, but certain fact, that in orchidaceous plants, forms just as different as wheat, barley, rye, and oats, have been proved by the most rigorous evidence, to be accidental variations of one common form, brought about no one knows how, but before our eyes, and rendered permanent by equally mysterious agency. The says Reason, if they occur in orchidaceous plants, why should they not also occur in corn plants? for it is not likely that such vagaries will be confined to one little group in the vegetable kingdom; it is more rational to believe them to be a part of the *general system* of creation. . . . . .How can we be *sure*, that wheat, rye, oats, and barley, are not all accidental off-sets from some unsuspected species?' "

It may be so; but this would only prove that the " unsuspected species" included greater varieties, not that a really defined species was transmutable into another. But it is a point upon which no satisfactory result can be arrived at; since naturalists are not agreed in the classification of species, nor what attributes constitute one.

The Broomfield experiment is again brought forward, as decisive of the power to originate new life from inorganic elements. It will be remembered that Mr. WEEKES, of Sandwich, continued during three years to subject solutions to electric action, and invariably found insects produced in these instances, while they as invariably failed to appear where the electric action was not employed, but every other condition fulfilled. In a letter to the author of the *Vestiges*—two are inserted, one on the independent generation of fungi—Mr. WEEKES says—

"One hundred and sixty-six days from the commencement of the experiment—the first acari seen in connexion therewith, six in number and nearly full-grown, were discovered on the outside of the open glass vessel. On removing two pieces of card which had been laid over the mouth of this vessel, several fine specimens were found inhabiting the under surfaces, and others completely developed and in active motion here and there within the glass. Making my visit at an hour when a more favourable light entered the room, swarms of acari were found on the cards, about the glass tumbler, both within and without, and also on the platform of the apparatus. At this identical hour Dr. J. Black favoured me with a call, inspected the arrangements, and received six living specimens of the acarus produced from solution in the open vessel."

Specimens of the insect were sent to Paris, when they set a whole conclave of philosophers a-laughing, because they were found to contain ova. Other specimens were sent to London, but there their fate was sealed by their being found to be, not a new species, but one then abundant in the country. For ourselves we think the experiment not conclusive. We adopt HUME's principle. All but universal experience having established that life is *ex ovo* only, we must have a proportionate body of counter evidence to establish a different mode of generation. At all events, Mr. WEEKES's protracted gestation of 166 days by his galvanic battery is not likely, in the existing rage for despatch, to supersede the existing routine of reproduction.

LONDON : PRINTED BY C. WHITING, BEAUFORT HOUSE, STRAND.

THE ATLAS,

A General Family Newspaper and Journal of Literature.

This Periodical, which may be justly called a Weekly Cyclopædia of Politics, Literature, Arts, and Science, is published every Saturday afternoon, in time for the post, containing the News of Saturday.

The Atlas

IS DIVIDED INTO TWO PRINCIPAL DEPARTMENTS,

NEWS AND LITERATURE,

And these are subdivided and classified with care and industry into heads of easy reference, so that each particular subject is preserved distinct and entire. The dimensions of the sheet, which folds into sixteen large quarto-sized pages, containing forty-eight columns, afford this classification facilities which few other publications possess.

News.

PARLIAMENTARY DEBATES reported on a scale of magnitude far exceeding other weekly Journals.

PARLIAMENTARY PAPERS, a digest of all Parliamentary documents of obvious reference and popular utility.

FOREIGN NEWS, the current events in foreign countries, arranged in the form of historical narrative, collated carefully from contemporary authorities, and distributed under the heads of the different countries and colonies to which they belong.

BRITISH NEWS, a clear epitome of all domestic occurrences, under the various heads of Public Meetings, Trade, Agriculture, Accidents and Offences, Police, Proceedings of the Courts of Law and Sessions, Court and Fashionable News, Church and University Intelligence, Military and Naval Affairs copiously given, the Money Market, and the miscellaneous news of the week up to midnight on Saturday. The Local News of Ireland and Scotland, under separate heads. In the conduct of this department of the ATLAS recourse is had to many exclusive sources of information, and correspondents have been established who furnish expressly the latest intelligence. The Gazettes and

Tables of Markets, and all matters interesting to the Commercial World, are especially attended to. Preserving an independence in its editorial capacity, the ATLAS affords a faithful reflection of the opinions and proceedings of all political parties.

The attention that is observed in the purity of language and selection of subjects, down to the minutest paragraph in the ATLAS, recommends it especially to the use of families and the guardians of youth; and the copious details it affords of Military and Naval Affairs, invest it with valuable attractions for the members of these professions, and the residents in the Colonies.

Literature.

The Contributions to this department are from the pens of Professors and Gentlemen of acknowledged reputation, and are classified under the following heads:—

1.—ORIGINAL ESSAYS ON MEN AND THINGS, embodying a lively commentary on passing events and men and manners.

2.—THEATRICAL CRITICISMS upon the written and acted Drama, in which both are reviewed in a spirit of truth and perfect candour.

3.—REVIEWS of all new works of ability, with numerous extracts. Independent and free from all literary and personal prejudices, the opinions of the Reviewers in the ATLAS may be consulted with confidence in their integrity.

4.—LITERARY MEMORANDA, notes of all novelties in literature abroad and at home, and summary criticisms on all works of minor importance.

5.—MUSIC AND MUSICIANS, or scientific criticisms on vocal and instrumental performers, operas, and new music, on the Continent as well as in England, with occasional engraved illustrations.

6.—FINE ARTS, Weekly notices of pictorial exhibitions, and critical descriptions of paintings, drawings, and engravings, with commentaries on all new works of art.

7.—SCIENTIFIC NOTICES, or descriptions of improvements in Mechanics and the experimental Sciences, illustrated occasionally by diagrams, with an account of New Patents, Meteorological Tables, Proceedings of Literary and Scientific Institutions, &c.

The Literary division of the ATLAS in the various branches has formed an era in the class of publications in which it ranks; and exhibits a remarkable union of the essential features of the more elaborate Reviews, with the popular and practical objects of the General Newspaper.

Published for the Proprietor, at the office, 6, Southampton-street, Strand, London.—Price Eight Pence. Orders received by all Newsmen throughout the Kingdom.

In one volume octavo. cloth lettered, price Five Shillings,

NATIONAL DISTRESS,

ITS CAUSES AND REMEDIES;

▲

Prize Essay

AS ORIGINALLY PUBLISHED IN " THE ATLAS."

By SAMUEL LAING, Esq., Jun.,

Late Fellow of St. John's, Cambridge.

PART I.

PART II.

PART III.

LONDON:

PUBLISHED BY LONGMAN AND CO.; SIMPKIN AND MARSHALL; AND WHITTAKER AND CO.

ALSO,

AT THE ATLAS OFFICE, 6, SOUTHAMPTON-STREET, STRAND.

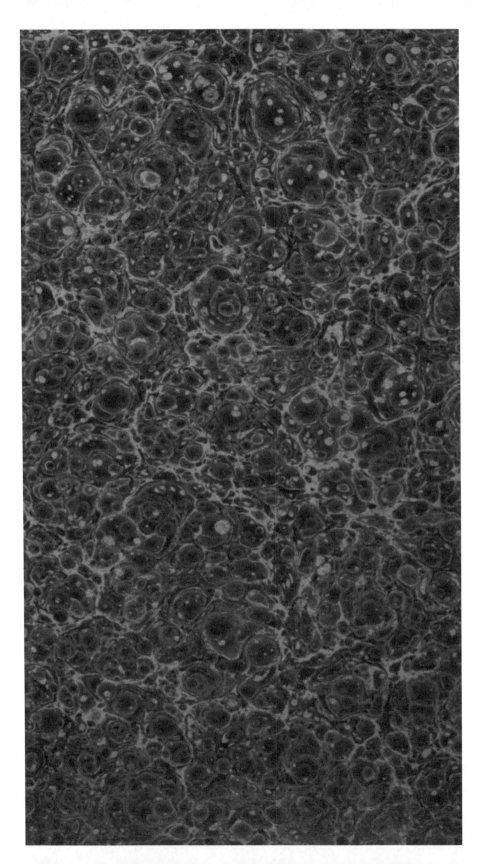